INFORMATION TECHNOLOGY: The Basics

City and Guilds Co-publishing Series

City and Guilds of London Institute has a long history of providing assessments and certification to those who have undertaken education and training in a wide variety of technical subjects or occupational areas. Its business is essentially to provide an assurance that pre-determined standards have been met. That activity has grown in importance over the past few years as government and national bodies strive to create the right conditions for the steady growth of a skilled and flexible workforce.

Both teachers and learners need materials to support them as they work towards the attainment of qualifications, and City and Guilds is pleased to be working with several distinguished publishers towards meeting that need. It has been closely involved in planning, author selection and text appraisal, although the opinions expressed in the publications are those of the individual authors and are not necessarily those of the Institute.

City and Guilds is fully committed to the projects listed below and is pleased to commend them to teaching staff, students and their advisers.

Carolyn Andrew and others. *Business Administration Level I* and *Business Administration Level II* (John Murray)

David Minton, *Teaching Skills in Further and Adult Education* (Macmillan)

Graham Morris and Lesley Reveler. *Retail Certificate Workbook* (Levels 1 and 2) (Macmillan)

Peter Riley (consultant editor). *Computer-aided Engineering* (Macmillan)

Barbara Wilson. *Information Technology: the Basics* (Macmillan)

Caroline Wilkinson. *Information Technology in the Office* (Macmillan)

INFORMATION TECHNOLOGY: The Basics

Barbara Wilson

Consultant editor: Chris West
Chief Executive, ECCTIS 2000

To the memory of my father, Philip Jeffs

First published 1992 by
THE MACMILLAN PRESS LTD
Houndmills, Basingstoke, Hampshire RG21 2XS
and London
Companies and representatives
throughout the world

ISBN 0–333–55714–X

A catalogue record for this book is available
from the British Library

Printed in Great Britain by Butler & Tanner, Frome, Somerset

10 9 8 7 6 5 4 3 2 1
01 00 99 98 97 96 95 94 93 92

CONTENTS

ACKNOWLEDGEMENTS

I am grateful to my family for all the support and encouragement they gave me while I was writing this book, in particular my husband David whose vast knowledge of computers and the English language were invaluable to me. I should also like to thank Perry Vincent of Afan College, Port Talbot, West Glamorgan, for his help and advice, Jean Macqueen who edited the text, and my many friends at South Trafford College for their support.

Thanks are also due to the following for permission to use copyright material:

Austin Rover (page 37); Barclays Banks PLC (page 28); Dairy Crest Ltd (page 11 right); Ford Motor Company (pages 23, 120); GEC Alstom (page 21); Hewlett Packard (pages 23, 32, 35); IBM UK Ltd (pages 4, 24); MANWEB PLC (page 26); Marks and Spencer PLC (page 25); Motorola Ltd (page 17 right); National Nuclear Corporation/Westinghouse (page 5); NCR Ltd (pages 22, 36); Chris Pearsall (page 11 left); Poly-Press, Cologne (page 17 left); Psion Ltd (page 12); Research Machines Ltd (pages 9, 22); Storagetek (page 41).

Every effort has been made to trace all the copyright holders, but if any have inadvertently been overlooked the publishers will be pleased to make the necessary arrangement at the first opportunity.

BARBARA WILSON

ABOUT THIS BOOK

WHO IT'S FOR

This book is a beginners' guide to information technology and the use of computers. Everything is explained and no previous knowledge is assumed, making it equally suitable for the 16- and the 80-year-old. It can be used by people on information technology courses in school and college or on company-based training courses, and by those working independently at home.

It covers the requirements of the City and Guilds 4242 scheme (Basic competence in IT) and the first-level modules on word processing, databases and spreadsheets of the 7261 IT scheme. It is also suitable for equivalent RSA and BTEC courses.

WHAT IT CONTAINS

The book is divided into ten chapters. The first six deal with the background needed to make you feel at ease with the machines, and introduces you to some of the words and terms you need to know. The rest of the book covers the most common applications of computers – word processing, databases, spreadsheets – and an introduction to computer-aided graphics and desk top publishing.

The approach is practical, and is concerned with getting you to learn by doing. Throughout the book there are sections marked TO DO. These include tasks and activities to help you become familiar with a computer system and use it to complete a wide range of practical exercises.

You will also see sections marked YOU SHOULD NOW BE ABLE TO. . . These list skills and knowledge which you should have at that particular stage in your learning. These will be useful in keeping track of your progress in building up competence. There are also sections marked with an elephant symbol: these summarise important information or points to note in that part of the book.

A Glossary explaining some of the most common words and terms is given at the end of the book.

HOW TO USE IT

The early parts of the book can be used without a computer, but to get the most out of it you will need access to a microcomputer system, including a printer, together with standard applications packages for word processing, databases, spreadsheets and graphics and desk top publishing. The exercises can all be done using any system and any package.

You will find it helpful to keep a notebook or file in which to keep a note of information you acquire from doing the activities. Further tasks on all the applications can be found in the companion book *Information Technology in the Office* by Caroline Wilkinson (also published by Macmillan in association with City and Guilds).

Now start reading this book and practising the activities. You will soon find that your confidence builds and your skills increase. Enjoy it!

WHAT IS INFORMATION TECHNOLOGY?

Let's make a start by looking at these two words: 'information' and 'technology'.

Information

Information is **data with meaning.**
This is best understood by looking at some examples of data (or facts) and information.

Suppose I told you that the temperature in London at noon on 3 August 1990 was 38°C. This is a fact or a piece of **data.** You would probably say, 'so what?'
    But if I added that the normal midday temperature in London in August is 20°C, then you would have a piece of information – it was very hot for London in August!

'Driveoff Garages sold 10 new cars on 1 August 1990.' This is a fact.

Now add a second statement:
    'Driveoff Garages sold 30 new cars on the same day in 1989.' This gives you the *information* that their sales have dropped.

TO DO

Decide which is data and which information in the following statement:
    'The cost of buying a pair of trainers from Budget Shoes is £20 but the cost at Shoestyle is £35.'

Technology

This can be defined as the application of science – in other words, the way in which science is used to help us in our everyday lives. For example, the scientific discoveries about the principles of flight allowed the technological development of the aeroplane.

- **Information technology** (IT for short) is the means by which science is used in the **collection, storage, processing and movement of information.**

You should now be able to:

☐ understand that information means something to the person using it – it is not just a piece of data.

WHY STUDY IT?

Today information plays an important part in our working and every-day lives. When you book a holiday you can choose from thousands of hotels at hundreds of different places. The assistant in the travel agency can check on the availability of rooms and flights within minutes. Without the use of IT this would take weeks, or a lot of very expensive phone calls.

Your pay slip and your exam result slip are probably both computer-produced. Your bank or building society statement certainly is. And how would we manage without those 'hole in the wall' computers that hand out money!

Remember that IT is there for people to use:

- the hotel receptionist taking room bookings
- the managing director making decisions on sales targets
- the small child producing their first poem beautifully printed out.

Everyone's life can be – and indeed already is – influenced by IT. (Did you know that if computers hadn't been invented, the banks would by now have had so much paperwork that they'd have employed the entire working population?) The more you know about IT, the easier you will find it to use the technology without fear and to understand that it is here as a tool for you to use to make your working life easier, and your leisure time more fun.

TO DO

Make a list of the ways in which you can see IT being used as you go through a day – at home, at work, shopping, at school or college.

WHAT IS A COMPUTER?

A computer is one of the machines that technology has given us to use in information handling. On their own computers can do nothing, but with people to give them instructions they are powerful and useful tools.

The first computers were so called because they were used simply to do sums or to compute results.

Since those early days, however, technology has advanced so much that computers can now be used as tools in many ways:

- as calculators
- as pen and paper
- as filing cabinets
- as reference books
- as teachers,

to mention just a few. The reason why they are so useful is that they do all these things electronically far faster than we can do them by hand.

You should now be able to understand:

☐ why you need to learn about IT.

Information = data + meaning

Technology is the use of science.

Information technology is the way in which science is used to collect, store, process and move information.

- **Most important: IT is for *you* to use to make life easier for *you*!**

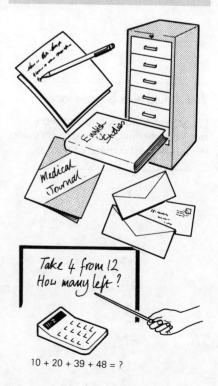

Take 4 from 12
How many left?

10 + 20 + 39 + 48 = ?

Look again at the list of things that computers are used for. It is easy to see that to do any of those jobs information must be **input** (given to the computer) and the computer will do something with it to produce **output** (what we want). It also needs to be given instructions as to what to do – it cannot think or act on its own. You will find out more about this later.

In the example in the drawing, the input is the numbers of different records being sold by all the record shops in the country, and the output is the current charts. What the computer does is to work out from all the information it has been given which records are the most popular. It does this processing in the way it has been told to.

Computers have several advantages over people:

- they don't get bored or distracted, so they can do the same job thousands of times very quickly (**speed**)
- they don't make mistakes, so they always get the same results from the same information (**accuracy and consistency**)
- they can remember large amount of information (**storage**)

Today computers come in many different shapes and sizes, from the pocket-held variety to desk top personal computers right through to the huge mainframe machines used by the very big information-processing organisations like insurance firms, councils and banks.

TO DO

Look at computer advertisements in magazines – not just the ones designed for computer users, but some of the business magazines too. Make a note of the manufacturers' names and see how often the different ones are mentioned. This will give you an idea of which makes are the most popular.

You should now be able to:

☐ understand that a computer is a tool that takes input and processes it to produce output

☐ understand that it will only do what we ask it to do

☐ realise that we need to give it information for it to produce results.

At one time it was easy to split computers into three groups according to their size:

micro   smallest

mini   ↓

mainframe   largest

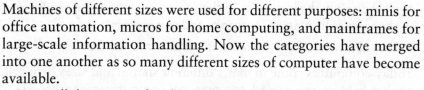

A large computer system
can fill a whole
room ...

... but this microcomputer sits on a single desk top

Machines of different sizes were used for different purposes: minis for office automation, micros for home computing, and mainframes for large-scale information handling. Now the categories have merged into one another as so many different sizes of computer have become available.

You will, however, often hear people talking about 'PCs'. PC simply stands for **personal computer**, a machine at the micro end of the scale, designed for use by an individual rather than by a large company or a group of people in an office.

Although most computers today can be used to do a variety of jobs, it is sometimes worth having a computer which does just one. This is usually because the job to be done is repetitive and boring, and so better suited to a computer than to a person. Or the job may be in a dangerous environment, or some risk may arise if it is not done accurately every time. Or it may just be the only job which is suitable for a computer to do in that particular place.

A computer that is designed and used for only one job is known as a **dedicated computer.**

You should now be able to:

☐ realise what advantages a computer has over humans

☐ understand some of the names given to computers.

Computers in use in the control room of Hinckley 'B' nuclear power station in Somerset

Part I

INTRODUCING COMPUTER SYSTEMS

1 · HOW IT WORKS

Once you have decided what job a computer can usefully do for you, the first thing you have to do is to get the information (input) you want to use into the computer. On the most common systems this is done by using a **keyboard**.

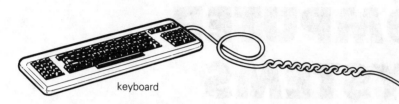

keyboard

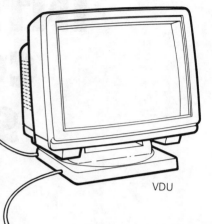

VDU

Information is **typed** or **keyed** in, and passes as a series of electrical impulses through wires running from the keyboard to the 'brain' or main part of the computer. This is called the **central processing unit** (CPU for short). In some machines the keyboard and processor are built in together in one box.

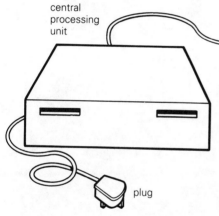

central
processing
unit

plug

You need to be able to see what you have typed in, and whether you have made any mistakes. So your typing is displayed on the screen of a **visual display unit** (VDU), sometimes called a **monitor**. The VDU is also used to show the information produced by the processor – the results or output of the jobs we have asked the computer to do. All computers need some source of electricity – either the mains supply (i.e. plugged in to a socket) or batteries fitted inside the machine itself.

TO DO

Look at your own computer system and identify the three main components. Follow the course of the wires and check that you know how the system is connected.

Most computer systems include a fourth component: extra information storage. The processor itself can store some information in its **internal memory**, but this is usually too small for most purposes.

> The three main components of a typical small computer system are:
> - a keyboard – for input
> - a processor – to do the work
> - a VDU – to display input and output.

disk drive

cassette

floppy disk

If you look at your own computer system you will probably be able to find a **disk drive**. It may be built into the same box as the processor, or it may be a separate unit. The disks it uses are known as **auxiliary** or **secondary storage** and are used to increase the available memory of the computer system. The processor's own memory is called the **primary storage**.

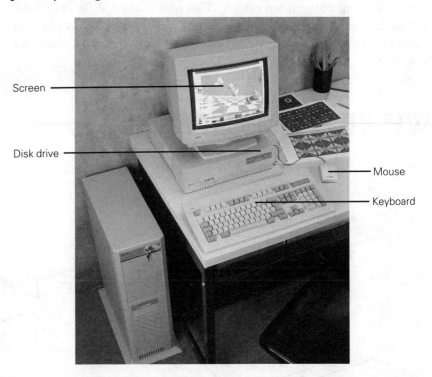

Screen

Disk drive

Mouse

Keyboard

When a computer is told to perform a job it will **load** (put into its **internal memory**) the instructions and data it needs to do that job. This is like the way you stand on the kerb recalling from the depths of your mind (your long-term memory) the procedures that you need to follow in order to cross the road.

Look right
Look left

This now gives us four main parts of a computer system:

- an input device – the keyboard
- an output device – the VDU
- a processor and
- auxiliary data storage – a disk drive or similar.

The central processing unit or CPU, mentioned above, is a complex piece of equipment. It is divided into different parts, each part performing a different job. For instance, there is a **control unit** which regulates the flow of information in, around and out of the processor and other parts of the system. There is the part where all the work is done, like adding up two numbers or comparing records of car registrations to find the owner of a stolen vehicle. This part of the CPU is called the **arithmetic and logic unit** (ALU). There are also areas known as **registers**, where the data and instructions waiting to be processed can be stored.

WHAT ELSE IS NEEDED?

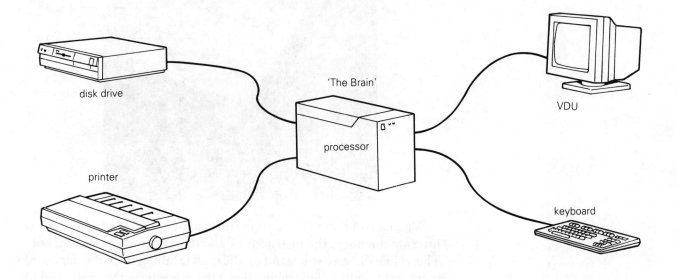

The processor is the most important part of a computer system. All the other devices – VDUs, keyboards, printers, disk drives and so forth – which are connected to it and controlled by it are peripheral units. All computer systems have a CPU, but the peripheral units attached to the CPU and controlled by it may be different.

Some peripheral units convert information from a form that humans understand into one which the computer can understand (input).

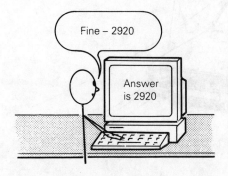

Other units convert computer-generated results into a human-understandable form (output).

Sometimes, however, this is not quite what is required. For instance, in a factory a computer-controlled machine is packing bottles into boxes. Signals have to be sent from the packing machine to the computer to allow it to count the number of bottles packed. More signals are sent from the computer to the bottle-packing machine to tell it when to move to the next space in the box or the next box. None of these signals or messages have to be sent in a form humans can understand. They are simply sent as data.

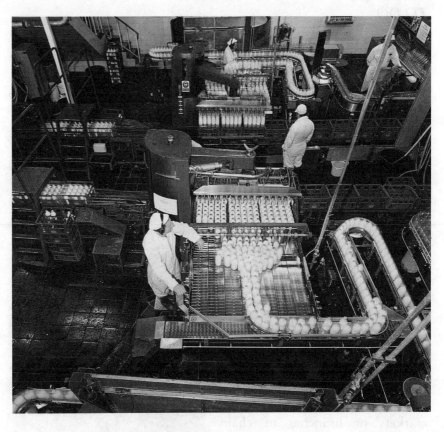

From milk tanker to crate, the processes in a large dairy are controlled from a central microprocessor unit (left); (right) the bottling hall

More complex computer systems are being produced all the time. It often happens now that information is processed first by one computer and then by another before being converted into human-understandable output through a peripheral device.

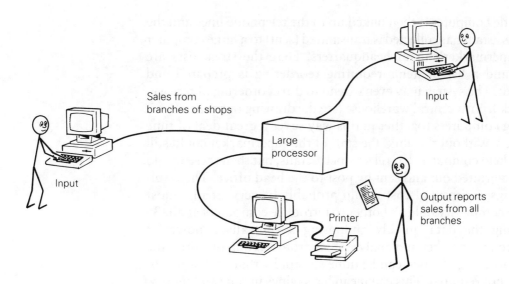

TO DO

Make a list of all the peripheral devices you see and why they are suitable for the use being made of them. Try to find examples from college or school, work and shops.

Make a list of the words printed in heavy type on the previous pages. Learn what they all mean.

WHY DO WE NEED SO MANY COMPUTERS?

On the previous pages you met the idea of computers 'talking' to one another. You have also seen that the great range of computers now available is a result of the different purposes for which people wish to use them.

Both of these are illustrated by the use of hand-held computers – you may have seen these in supermarkets or branches of chain stores.

You should now be able to:

☐ identify different types of input and output devices, and understand why they are being used.

A hand-held computer that can be used in many different ways

An assistant goes round the store recording the number of packets of say, different types of biscuits, and records this on a hand-held computer.

This little computer is then linked up to the telephone lines and the data the assistant has collected is transmitted (sent) to a large computer at the supermarket's main headquarters. Here the stock lists are updated and a list of items requiring reordering is prepared and printed out. The system may even extend to direct ordering of replacement stock from a central warehouse (see the drawing opposite).

Linking computers together in this way saves a great deal of time and money. Without this link, the staff of the supermarket could still use hand-held computers to collect stock details, but then these would have to be printed out and sent by post to the head office. The resultant savings in time and cost would probably be very small – most likely, the company wouldn't bother to introduce computers at all. By transferring the data quickly and using a centralised powerful machine to put together and analyse stock from a group of stores, the actual reordering of stock can be done so rapidly that vast stores of goods are not required. This can mean big savings in time and money, since the need for warehousing and storage space is much reduced. The ability to link computers together like this has led to a dramatic increase in the number of possible uses for them.

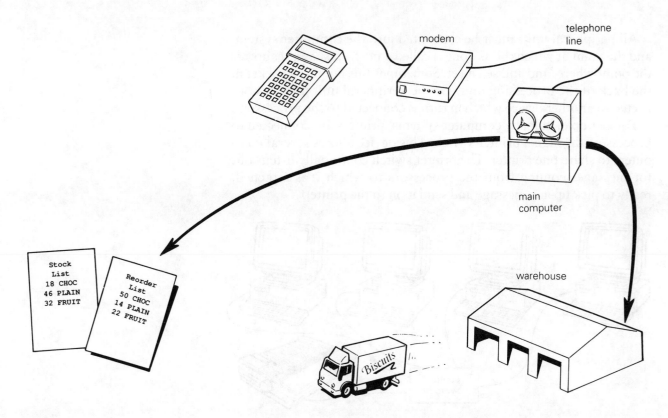

People normally only use computers if they

- save money, or
- save time (and usually, in the end, money) or
- are needed for something that humans would find dangerous.

TO DO

When you next go shopping, see if you can see any evidence of a computerised stock control system being used.

CONNECTIONS

With any computer system it is important that all the units can understand one another (are **compatible**) and are listening at the same time.

If you are speaking down the telephone in English and the person at the other end can only understand French, you will get nowhere.

Similarly, if your caller can understand English but isn't actually listening when you answer, nothing will happen.

All peripheral units must be connected into the computer system, and the point at which this is done is called a **port** – just as a seaport is the point where land and sea meet. Sometimes this point is a socket in the back of the processing unit. Or the peripheral unit may be connected to another device which in turn is connected to the processor.

For example, in many computer systems, printers are connected to processors through a **printer switch**. This device allows several computers to share one printer. The printer switch continually listens out for messages coming from the processors to which it is attached, ready to pick up any message and send it on to the printer.

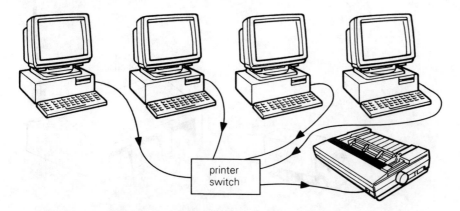

When the computer is listening to an input device, or an output device is ready waiting for the computer to send it instructions, then the device is said to be **on line**. But a device that is not listening is said to be **off line** – just like the person at the end of the telephone line!

TO DO (1)

Look at a computer system you use and see if you can recognise the ports. You will need to look at the back of the processor. You will probably need to get someone to show you what to look for.

TO DO (2)

Next time you or someone you know uses a cash machine, try to think about what is happening. How quickly do you think the information and instructions are being dealt with?

The peripheral devices and the processor itself are called **hardware** – they are physical objects that we can see. The instructions that make them work are called **software**. The software in the processor allows it to use and understand peripheral units attached to it. For example, have you ever heard someone saying, 'this computer isn't set up to use that printer'? This means that the software is not there to allow the processor to send messages the printer can understand. It's just like people speaking in different languages without a translator. In the case of a processor and a printer the software acts as the translator.

WHAT IS MEMORY?

On page 8 you read about the central processor and the fact that part of it contains the **memory** of the computer system. This is one area where the development of computer systems has been very active.

The early computers had hardly any memory. They had to be given instructions and data piece by piece, which meant they were not very efficient. Now the data and instructions can be stored in registers within the computer's memory ready for when they are needed.

The size of the processor's memory determines what type of programs (instructions) we can use it for, and how much data it can handle.

So how does this memory work?

A computer cannot understand letters or numbers. Any instruction or piece of data has to be coded or **translated** into a form that the computer can understand. Since computers work on electricity, the code that is used is based on whether an electrical impulse is present or absent – just like an electric switch, which can be either on or off.

In computers these impulses are known as **binary digits** or **bits**.

Each bit can be given one of two values, according to whether the electrical impulse is on or not. So we can only represent something which has two values – true or false, for example. Usually the numbers 0 and 1 are used.

If we use two bits we have more possibilities:

$$00 \qquad 01 \qquad 10 \qquad 11$$

So we could use these to code the four numbers 0, 1, 2 and 3.

With three bits we have eight possible codes:

$$000 \quad 001 \quad 010 \quad 011 \quad 100 \quad 101 \quad 110 \quad 111$$

These could be used for coding the numbers from 0 to 7.

If you like maths, you will have noticed that we are increasing the number of codes each time by a factor of 2. That is:

1 bit gives us 2 codes
2 bits 2×2 codes
3 bits $2 \times 2 \times 2$ codes
n bits 2^n codes

The number of possible codes = 2^n, where n is the number of bits used.

TO DO

On your keyboard there are all the letters of the alphabet, which can be either small or capitals. There are also the numbers 0 to 9, and a lot of other symbols such as '?', '£' and so on. Can you work out how many bits are needed to provide enough codes for each of the symbols on your keyboard?

Most computer systems today work by using 8 bits to represent a single letter or character. The reason for this is that 8 bits give us a total of 256 different codes, sufficient to represent all the letters of the alphabet (large and small), arithmetic signs, punctuation marks and a few special characters as well.

Eight bits combined together into one unit are called a byte. So, for example, the letter 'a' may be represented by the byte 01100001, and the sign '?' by the byte 00111111.

The actual form of these depends on the code the particular computer uses. Probably the most common code is the ASCII code (see p.128). The codes shown above are ASCII codes.

If one byte is used to represent one letter, then clearly the word 'round' would need 5 bytes or 40 bits. Look at the sentence:

The world is round.

This sentence would need 19 bytes (this includes the bytes required to show spaces and the full stop) or $19 \times 8 = 152$ bits.

TO DO

Work out how many bytes, and how many bits, would be needed to represent your name and address.

Step 1 Calculate how many characters (numbers, letters, punctuation marks and spaces) there are in your name and address – work this out line by line. This will give you the number of *bytes* you need.

Step 2 Then multiply the number of characters by 8 to give the number of *bits* needed.

As you can see, a processor needs a lot of bytes of memory to store even simple instructions or pieces of data. This is why you see computers advertised with memory sizes measured in kilobytes (1 kb = about 10^2 bytes – to be exact, 1024 bytes), megabytes (1 Mb = about 10^6 bytes) or even gigabytes (1 gb = around 10^9 bytes)!

A description of a PC might include the words 'it has an 8 bit 640k processor'. This means the processor has the space in its memory to store 640×1024 characters, each represented by 8 bits.

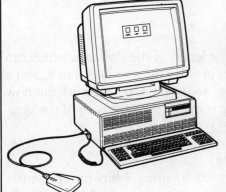

Look in magazines and in shops and see how computers are described in the advertisements. Collect information on the different computers you see under the following headings:

Make	Model	Memory size	Cost

Where is the memory in a computer system?

The simple answer is – on a **chip**!

This is another term that you will probably have heard mentioned when people talk about computers (or a lot of other electronic gadgets about today). A chip is a small, thin slice of (usually) silicon, on which have been added electronic circuits. The term **microchip technology** simply refers to the use of these small units in the control of many pieces of equipment. One familiar example is the automatic washing machine.

A processor in a computer system may be just one chip, or made up of a number of chips. If there is just one then the computer is known as a 'single chip computer' and the chip will be divided into different areas, each used for a different purpose, with one part used for the memory. Single chip machines are used in calculators and microwave ovens.

The more powerful the computer, or the faster it runs, the greater the number of chips used or the more densely packed are the electronic circuits on each chip. (There is a limit to this packing, however. If the circuits are too close too much heat is generated, and interference between the circuits is caused.)

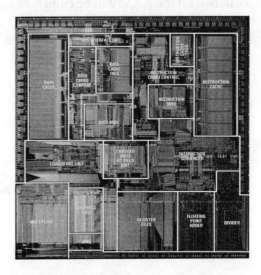

A microchip compared with the size of a hand (left) and detail of the Motorola microprocessor MC88110 (right).

In these multichip machines, some of the chips will be used solely for the processor's memory.

RAM AND ROM

There are two kinds of computer memory, both of which contain coded data or instructions. These are known as ROM and RAM, for short.

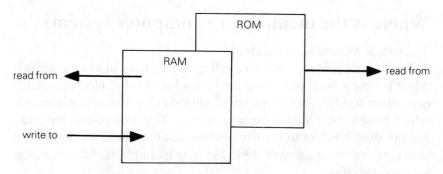

ROM or Read Only Memory

This part of the computer's memory contains instructions and information which are put into the processor when it is manufactured. As computer users we cannot alter this memory and when we use it we can only **read** from it. Every time the computer is switched on the information in the ROM becomes available. The ROM is stored on one or more chips.

RAM or Random Access Memory

This is the memory which is used to store data or instructions that you give to the computer. It is carried on one or more chips. Unlike ROM, the RAM can be both **read from** and **written to**. The information in RAM will only stay there while the computer is on, however – it is lost as soon as the power supply goes. The next time the computer is switched on the RAM will be empty: none of the information that was held in the RAM will still be there.

You can think of the RAM as being like a wipeable noteboard which is used and then wiped clean.

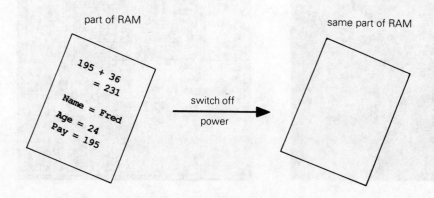

Many people get caught out when they are starting to use computers because they think that once they have 'keyed in' data it will always be there in the computer's memory. This is definitely *not* true! If you lose your power supply while you are working, everything in the RAM will be lost.

The memory is called 'random access memory' because the computer can access information from *any* position within it. It does not have to keep reading the information in the order in which it was put in, or writing to it in any given order either. It simply fills information into the first available free space. The opposite of random access is **serial access**.

Computers are being improved all the time. Sometimes it even seems as if they are becoming a bit like humans!

You may have seen films that show computers as being 'super-human' machines, able to talk and answer questions. This can be very misleading! It is important to remember that computers are only as clever as the people who use them.

All the same, in the development of input devices you can see how little by little the computers of today do behave just a bit like humans.

INPUT

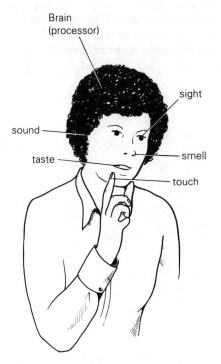

We use our own senses as input devices to send messages to our processors – our brains

All input devices are designed to get the information into the computer in the best possible way, just as we use certain of our senses in different situations. For instance, if we want to read a book then we use our eyes as the input mechanism. If we listen to a record, then we use our ears as the input device.

In this way different input devices have been developed to make data input as efficient as possible. The older data input devices relied on **mechanical processes**. But these are so much slower than the **electrical processes** that the computer uses that they slow down the overall **throughput** of a computer system. Modern input devices use a variety of techniques based on the human senses and their development has resulted in the increasing number of situations in which computers are used.

On the next few pages are details of some of the most common input methods, divided up into groups according to the human senses they most closely represent.

Mechanical processes are ones where things move. For example, a key is pressed down on a keyboard or a 'mouse' (see page 22) is moved across a table.

Electrical processes are much faster. Just compare the time it takes for you to find and press a switch with the time it takes for the electricity actually to reach a light bulb.

TOUCH

Keyboards

Keyboards are based on the typewriter keyboard with which most people are familiar, and use the same letters, numbers and other characters that are used in handwritten communications.

The physical movements of the keys are translated into electrical signals that the processor understands. The most widely used keyboard is the so-called QWERTY keyboard – a name based on the position of the keys on the keyboard. (Have a look at yours to see if it is one of these.)

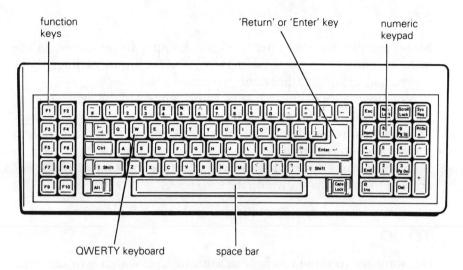

function keys 'Return' or 'Enter' key numeric keypad

QWERTY keyboard space bar

There are, however, many different types of keyboard in use today. Some of them have a restricted number of keys, such as the numeric **keypads** which are often used for recording stock in a warehouse, or to restrict entry through doors to a secure area of an office.

Some special keyboards have raised letters in Braille on them for blind people to use. Some have special larger keys, for other physically disabled people.

Joysticks

You probably already know what a joystick is. You may associate it with playing computer games, or with the original joysticks used to control the early aeroplanes.

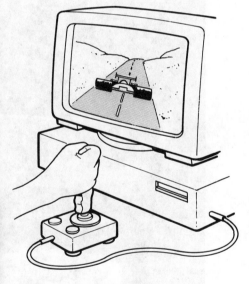

The principle is the same. The physical movement of the joystick is translated into the movement on a computer screen of an object or of another device to which the processor is connected. For

instance, you might be steering a car in a computer game or checking the size of a machine tool part using a computer-controlled measuring machine, as shown in the photograph.

Often the cursor keys on the keyboard are used instead of a joystick.

Mice

Many computer systems are used for design – for example, in the fashion industry – and these may require the input of lines, both curved and straight, rather than characters or numbers.

A mouse is a small device (see picture), connected through a port to the processor. As it is moved gently across a table top or mouse pad, its movement is translated into lines on the screen by the controlling software or **mouse driver**.

A mouse can also be used to move a cursor to point at and select options from menus shown on the screen.

A mouse for the computer

TO DO

Get someone to show you how to use a mouse. Watch how carefully you need to move it.

Find out if you can attach a mouse to the machine you will be using.

Touch-sensitive screens

A touch-sensitive screen is exactly what its name suggests – if you touch the screen with your finger then the information on the part of the screen that you have touched is picked up by the processor as input.

A touch-sensitive screen

Electronic digitisers

These are often used by people producing maps or technical drawings. A device (called a **puck**) is moved across a special screen or tablet. Its track is recorded as a series of co-ordinates, representing its position at successive instants of time. These are stored by the processor.

An electronic digitiser in use by a car body designer

Pressure digitisers

These are the most recently developed input devices based on touch. They are designed to be able to accept handwritten entry.

A special pen and writing tablet are used. You write directly on to the tablet, and the letters and their position are recorded for storing, moving about or printing. The different letters are recognised by the changing pressure of the special pen on the pad.

Pressure digitisers are already in use for signature recognition, and can be used to pick up printed characters. They could be an ideal form of input device: a handwritten message can be stored electronically, filed away, transmitted thousands of miles or converted into a typed letter as required.

You should now be able to:

☐ recognise all the input devices described so far and understand why they have been developed.

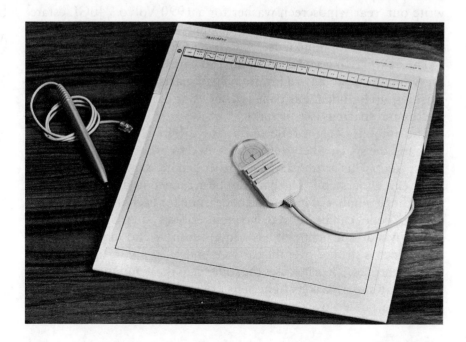

A pressure digitiser, with its accessories

As you work through this section, make a table summarising your knowledge of input devices under the following headings:

Device	Sense based on	Typical use	Advantages or disadvantages

SIGHT

Humans use reflected light to see objects, and to recognise printed characters and pictures on different background material.

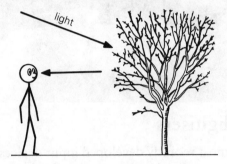

Light travels much more quickly than any physical object can. So input devices that use light work faster than those using physical movements. The development of such devices has been coupled with the development of special **input documents** and **input codes** designed with the computer in mind. These are described below.

Optical mark recognition (OMR)

Since computers cannot handle letters, these have to be coded for them. Humans often convert things into codes to make life easier for themselves, too. For instance, most cars have model numbers and their spare parts have code numbers too. So assistants don't have to write out 'rear windscreen washer for a 1990 Volvo 740GL estate' every time they sell one! So why not arrange for computers to use the codes that exist for human use?

This is where **bar codes** come in. You can see bar codes on nearly everything you can buy today, from spare parts for cars to a bottle of washing-up liquid. A bar code is a series of dark bands of different widths and spacings (see picture).

The amount of light reflected by the different thicknesses of the bars and the spacing between them is used to produce a varying electric current. This is 'translated' into a coded message which the computer can understand. The bars can be arranged in different ways to give a huge number of individual codes, one for each item.

These codes can be input to a computerised system by using a **light pen** or **wand**. The light pen has a light-sensitive end (a photoelectric cell), which is stroked over the bar code and picks up the light reflected from the stripes. Then it passes the code on to the computer.

In many supermarkets light pens are no longer used. Instead, the goods are passed over a light-sensitive cell built into the counter

A bar code

A bar code reader in use at a supermarket checkout

surface beside the till. A bleep sounds as the operator passes each object over it and the cell 'reads' the code. If the code is not picked up a different sound is heard and the operator can try again, or enter the code manually.

A bar code reader incorporating a light-sensitive cell, built into a shop checkout

This type of terminal is also known as an **electronic point of sale** or **EPOS** terminal. It records all the details of the sale automatically as the sale is made.

There goes another baked bean tin

only another 2000 left in stock

Bar codes are just one example of the use of optical marks.

TO DO (1)

Go to a local shop or supermarket and make a list of all the different types of goods you can find with bar codes on. Try to look at a variety of things – clothes, footwear, books, food and household goods.

TO DO (2)

How do you think stocktaking and reordering of stock were done before bar codes were used? Try to find out how these are done in a shop near you.

Optical character recognition (OCR)

Input devices have now been developed that can identify characters rather than just marks. An example of a typical bill is shown overleaf, together with the payment slip that is used when the bill is paid.

Look carefully, and you will see that some of the information has been printed on to the payment slip so that it can easily be read off again when the slip is returned for payment. This is done using a special ink.

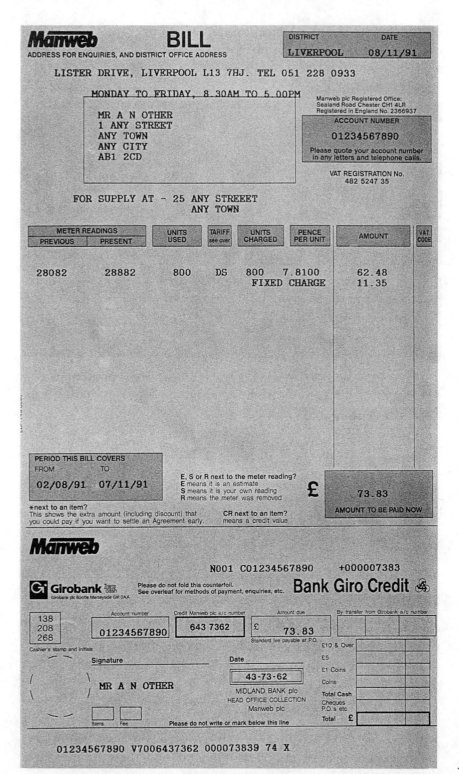

A turnaround document using OCR

This type of document, which is the *output* from one computerised system and will be the *input* to another, is known as a **turnaround document**.

TO DO

Have a look at bills which you see at home and see if you can recognise any of these turnaround documents.

What type of information looks as if it is in special ink?

This example shows how special documents have to be designed for collecting and inputting information into a computer. The exact position of the information to be picked up by the optical mark (or character) reader on the payment slip will have been carefully worked out. So will the design of the areas that have to be read by someone typing in the details using a keyboard.

Image processors or scanners

These devices scan a complete document or picture and input its image as a series of bits into the computer system, so that it can be stored, recalled or changed as required. They are commonly used with desk top publishing applications (see page 125) but their potential uses are far greater. It is technically possible to input and store *any* document in this way. For example, an insurance company could use scanners to build up complete files of all claims, letters and so forth.

This sort of system really can empty an office of paper! But it does need to use very efficient storage methods for the images. This generally requires the use of optical disks (see page 42) which are still rather expensive.

MAGNETIC INPUT

So far we have looked at input devices which work on touch and light. One type which doesn't fit easily into our comparison with human input methods is computer input based on magnetism.

Magnetic ink character recognition (MICR)

It is always convenient to use input devices that can recognise a set of marks that can also be understood by humans. Before optical character recognition systems were developed, input devices based on the principles of magnetism came into use. These could recognise characters printed on documents in special 'magnetic' ink. The documents had to be passed through a magnetic field before being read by the magnetic character reader.

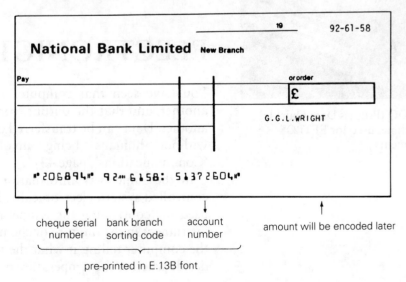

A bank cheque: the numerical codes along the lower edge are printed in magnetic ink

A cash card – front and back

They were first developed for use in banks in the USA, and soon became used throughout the British banking system on cheques.

Magnetic card reader

Magnetism is also used in bank **cash cards**, and other similar plastic cards. A magnetic card reader reads off details from the strip on the card.

Most people today have some form of plastic card, usually issued by a bank or a building society, which they can use to withdraw money or to find out how much they have in their accounts at a 'hole in the wall'.

These cards carry a magnetic strip which contains coded information about the account holder and his or her PIN (Personal Identification Number). When you want to withdraw money you have to put your card into a slot and then type in your PIN. The machine then compares the PIN with the details read off the card by the magnetic card reader.

TO DO

Look at a cheque and see if you can identify the characters that are to be read magnetically. Notice how the numbers differ from 'normal' numbers.

A bank service till

Magnetic card readers are also used in shops for payments using **credit cards**.

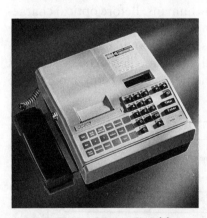

A PDQ (Process Data Quickly) machine, used for EFTPOS payments

The type of terminal shown in the picture is called an EFTPOS terminal, which stands for **Electronic Funds Transfer at Point of Sale**. This is a rather grand way of saying that 'money' is moved electronically (by computer) from a customer's bank account to a shop's account. The only physical objects to appear are pieces of paper – receipts; no actual coins or notes change hands.

ELECTRONIC INPUT

You have seen that computer systems quite often 'talk' to one another, and that the output from one system may be the input to another. Data can be transferred electronically, still in a coded form, without humans being involved at all (see Chapter 5, 'Communications', page 43).

In the same way information can be input into a computer-controlled system electronically. For instance, computers are often used for controlling the temperature of a chemical processes. An instrument in the mixture of chemicals will send electronic signals to the computer telling it what the temperature is. The computer will decide whether the temperature needs to be increased or decreased. It

Hint – Many of the words which people use when talking about computer systems sound complicated, but if you think of them in terms of what people do then they become much easier to understand.

Computers are after all only doing jobs which humans themselves used to do!

You should now be able to:

☐ understand which human input methods common input devices are based on

☐ understand the situations in which the different input devices are used

☐ have an idea of where developments in input devices are going

☐ recognise turnaround documents and characters which have been designed for computer input.

will then send signals electronically to the furnace, or perhaps to cooling fans to adjust the temperature as required.

THE FUTURE

People are basically lazy! The easier it is for them to use a computer, the more likely they are to use one.

Having moved from writing symbols or pictures to letters and then to words, which we first printed and then wrote in joined-up script, most people find it hard to make the transition backwards to typing in individual letters. And never mind the fact that for all but the fastest typist, keying-in information is a slow and error-prone method of communication!

If we could write in our normal longhand, wouldn't computers seem much more attractive? Even better, if only we could talk to them!

Voice input would provide the fastest form of input directly from a human to a machine.

As you know, computers need everything explaining to them very simply. In order to teach them how to recognise spoken instructions, they have first to be taught how the sounds humans make are made up. So scientists are now spending a great deal of time studying human voice patterns and breaking them up into chunks that the computer can manage.

There are many problems with this. For example, people often run words together when they speak, and they have a whole range of accents. And many words have more than one meaning!

Computers are already being used to recognise people's voice patterns to control access to high-security areas. Perhaps some of the predictions of science fiction films are not so far away after all!

TO DO

Answer the following questions:

1 Why are there so many different types of input device?

2 Which input devices are the most recent ones?

3 Why are there problems in developing voice input methods?

4 Which input device could really help to create 'a paperless office'?

5 What is special about the banks and their use of technology?

6 Why do we need input devices and what do they do?

3 · GETTING DATA OUT

VDU SCREENS

Probably the most common form of output device used is the VDU (often called a **monitor**). Almost every computer system includes a VDU, which can be used to show in human-understandable form not only the output from the processor, but the input which is necessary for the processor to work. It is *not* an input device: it just shows what has been entered and allows the operator to spot any mistakes.

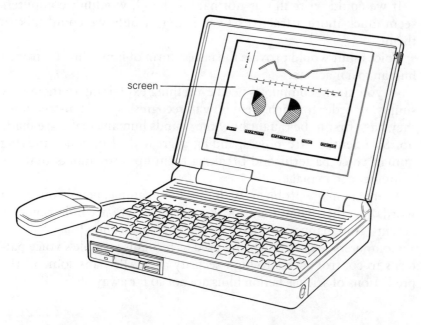

screen

The VDU screen of a portable computer is a flat panel let into the lid of the machine

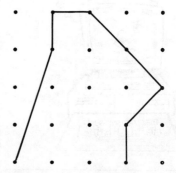

VDUs come in a variety of shapes and sizes and can be either **mono** (single colour on a different coloured background) or **colour**. The screen may be either tall and thin (**portrait**) or short and wide (**landscape**). The screens of portable PCs tend to be much smaller than those of desk top models.

Resolution

Screens are basically made up of a series of dots or **pixels,** and the more of these there are on the screen the better the **resolution** or quality of the pictures or letters. Look at the two 'dot to dot' pictures. You can see that the one at the top shows only a vague outline, whereas the one below gives a clearer image. The special high-quality screens used for graphics in design work have very high **pixel densities** (the dots are very close together).

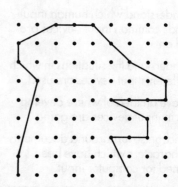

Colour

Mono screens are based on one colour only, using different shades of the one colour. Some use blue, others green or orange. Colour screens can use a great range of colours.

Sometimes instead of having coloured letters on a white background colours are reversed, so that white characters are seen on a coloured ground. This is called **reverse video**. The choice of screen is generally a question of money. The better the screen the more it costs, and it is only when a high-quality colour screen is essential for the type of work that the cost is justified. Usually a simple colour screen will do. Nowadays many programs use colours for highlighting instructions and messages, which just don't show up as clearly on a mono screen.

Flicker

Watching a flickering image on the screen is very bad for your eyes. A television screen used as a monitor often shows particularly bad flicker. Properly designed computer screens are much better.

Developments in screens

Screens based on the same principles as the television screen are bulky and often not suitable for working at for hours on end. Much research is being done in this area, and several different types of screen are now available. These are:

- gas plasma, as used in some calculators and petrol pumps
- LED, which stands for **light emitting diodes**; these are used in some calculators but are not good in bright natural light
- LCD, which stands for **liquid crystal display**; again these are used in calculators and in some portable computers, but the quality still needs improving.

TO DO (1)

Look at advertisements for computers and VDUs. See if you can find out the differences in price between different types of screen, such as colour/mono, LCD/plasma.

Find out the difference between VGA and EGA colour screens.

TO DO (2)

Try using the same program on different VDUs, a mono and a colour one. Which do you prefer? Do you find one colour of mono display easier on your eyes than another? Many people do.

Find the brightness and contrast controls on your VDU and try experimenting until you find the setting that best suits your eyes.

PRINTERS

Like screens, printers produce something you can look at. They have the advantage over screens, that their output lasts even after the computer system is switched off.

In simple terms, a printer is a device which when connected to a computer processor accepts electrical codes from the processor and converts them to produce printed words and characters which humans can understand. This printer output is often called **hard copy**.

Printers have developed considerably over the years, and new features have been introduced in response to changes in the demand for different types of output.

A laser printer, showing the single sheet feeder

Printers use paper of different shapes and sizes. Some of it comes in **single sheets** and some of it is **continuous**. Some continuous paper comes as a roll, with or without perforations. Some is **fan-folded** into sheets which are perforated so that they can easily be torn off. Paper comes in different widths, and printers are often described as being either **wide-bodied** or **narrow-bodied** depending on the width of paper that they can take. Many firms use specialised paper with things pre-printed on it, such as a company heading or pre-drawn boxes, or paper with characters pre-printed using special inks which are to be used at a later time for input into OCR or MICR readers (the turn-around documents mentioned on page 26).

There are two ways of feeding paper into a printer.

● With **friction feed**, the paper is gripped between two rollers, just as in a typewriter. This method is suitable for single sheets of paper. If a **cut sheet feeder** or **form feed** is attached to the printer, this will automatically feed sheets of paper into the friction feed mechanism.

● With **traction feed**, you have to use specially designed paper. This has holes along its sides, which fit over spokes on wheels at the side of a roller. The paper is dragged through the printer by the wheels. This method is used with continuous paper.

Many printers allow you to use a variety of paper sizes and you can select the type of feeding mechanism you wish to use.

Printers can be classified in several ways but the most common grouping is into 'impact' and 'non-impact' printers.

In **impact printers**, a printhead strikes the paper through a ribbon which contains ink (just like a typewriter works). These printers are mechanical, but some of them are still quite fast. They can be designed to give a very high quality of print.

Non-impact printers use a variety of techniques to produce the characters on paper. All of them aim to produce faster printing, or better-quality printed characters, or both.

There is a very wide variety of printers for sale, and the purpose for which the printer is going to be used is the most important factor to consider when buying one. For example, you may need a printer that can give you a variety of styles of letter (fonts) or you may be happy with just one.

Dot matrix printers (impact)

The characters produced by these printers are formed from a number of dots, made by tiny wires that strike the paper through the ribbon. The quality of the characters depends on the numbers of wires on the printhead, which can be anything up to 132. They are good general-purpose printers.

Some dot matrix printers have two settings: one 'draft', which gives very fast output of rather poor quality, and one 'NLQ' (near letter quality), giving better-quality output much more slowly.

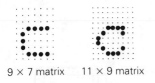

9 × 7 matrix   11 × 9 matrix

A character produced on a matrix grid

Daisywheel printers (impact)

These produce the same quality of print as an electric typewriter. Each of the spokes of a rapidly rotating wheel carries a single character at its tip, and these are made to strike the paper through the ribbon. They are used where a better quality of print required – for business letters, for example.

Ink jet (non-impact)

These work by squirting fine jets of ink on to the paper. They are useful for producing coloured output but are generally fairly slow.

Laser printers (non-impact)

These work something like a photocopier. They produce very high-quality output but operate fairly slowly.

TO DO (1)

Have a look at as many different types of printer as you can. Draw up a table like this one (we have put in details of one printer, as an example):

Make	Type	Use	Advantages or disadvantages
NEC Silentwriter2	Laser	High-quality letters etc	6 pages/minute Expensive (£1895)

TO DO (2)

Find out what type of printer you will be using. Make sure you know how to switch it on and off and what type of paper is used with it.

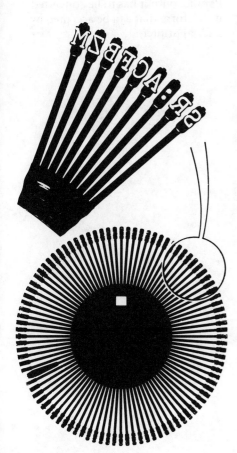

A daisy wheel

Get someone to demonstrate to you how to load your printer both with single sheet paper and with continuous feed paper.

Look at your printer to see the different feeding mechanisms for the paper, and whether it has NLQ and draft settings.

Serial and parallel printers

If you are choosing a printer to attach to your computer system you must be careful to choose one which is **compatible**, i.e. one that can understand the messages produced by your system and work with it.

The ports where you plug your printer into your processor can be either **serial ports** or **parallel ports**. Which they are depends on the design of the computer. The ports on the processor and the plugs on the printer cables will be different for parallel and serial devices.

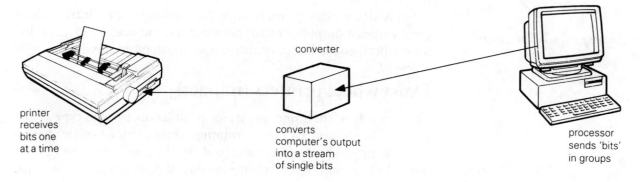

converter

printer receives bits one at a time

converts computer's output into a stream of single bits

processor sends 'bits' in groups

Parallel output has to be converted into a form that can be accepted by a serial printer

Why is the difference important?

Remember that computers deal with information in the form of bits, with usually eight bits needed to code one letter or character. A serial port can only deal with one bit at a time so the eight bits of a character have to be sent out one by one. A parallel port can cope with sending out several bits at one time.

A serial printer can only accept one bit at a time, but a parallel printer accepts a group of bits at a time. The result is simply that parallel printers are faster – just as traffic moves faster on a motorway with several lanes than in a narrow street.

If you do wish to connect a serial printer to a parallel port, or a parallel printer to a serial port, then you have to use a special device to convert from one method of transmitting data to the other. Again it is all a matter of translating codes, so that all parts of the computer system can understand one another.

OTHER OUTPUT DEVICES

There are other devices for output from computer systems but not as many as for input. This is because output from computer systems usually has to be understood by humans, whereas input can come from a variety of sources – not just directly from people.

VISUAL OUTPUT

Plotters

Printers produce printed characters and symbols on a page. But **plotters** can produce plans, maps, graphs or even pictures. For example, a plotter might be used in an architect's office for producing plans for wiring in buildings, or drainage systems on a building site. There are two types of plotter.

- In a **flat bed** plotter, a pen or pens move across and down a sheet of paper mounted on the plotter. It may be positioned either horizontally or vertically.
- In a **drum plotter** the paper is held on a drum, which can turn. As it does so, the pen moves across the paper.

Plotters can produce output of various qualities. The most expensive can produce high-quality drawings in colour.

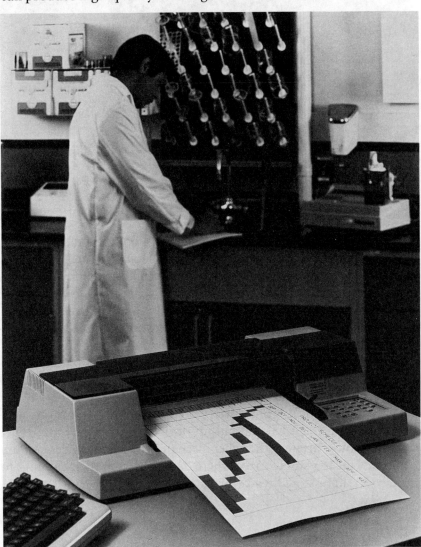

A plotter being used to produce graphical output in a laboratory

COM (computer output to microfilm/fiche)

If you go to your local library and ask for a book you cannot find on the shelves, the librarian will probably look it up in a **microfiche** catalogue. This is basically writing which has been greatly reduced in size

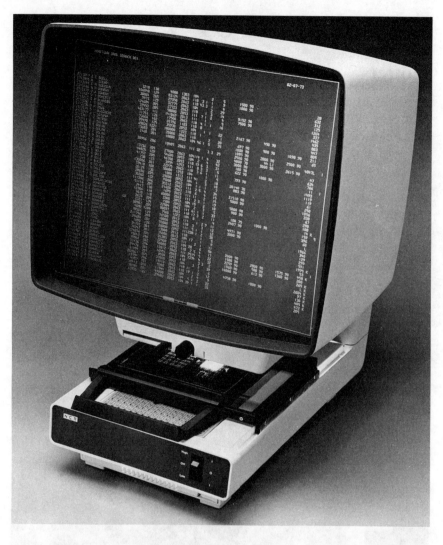

A microfiche reader used in a bank

and printed on to film or fiche (card-shaped pieces of film) which can be read by a special microfiche reader with a powerful magnifier. This condensed form of saving output from a computer system is also used for other large catalogues – for example, of spare parts in a garage or engineering works – or for **archiving** material which is no longer in everyday use but which has to be kept for research or audit (accounting) needs.

Microfilm (and microfiche) is one of the few ways in which computer-produced output has actually reduced the amount of paper in offices. All too often, people keep a paper copy – just in case!

Just as mechanical input devices are much slower than the electronic computer, mechanical output devices are slower too. To get round this most printers and other mechanical output devices contain a **buffer**. This is a storage area where data sent from the computer to the device can be stored ready for output.

TO DO

Watch what happens next time you print something out.

Does the computer tell you that printing has finished *before* the printer has actually printed everything out?

SOUND OUTPUT

This is much more common than voice or sound input, and its use is more advanced. Typical examples are:

- talking clocks
- travel announcements
- responses to routine telephone enquiries, such as the numbers given by BT's directory enquiries service
- warning voices in cars.

It is comparatively easy to produce voice output, as what is required is known in advance and therefore much easier to **simulate**.

ELECTRONIC OUTPUT

In the same way that one computer can receive electronic signals directly as input, output can be sent from one machine to another. Sometimes the output may not be to another computer but to a different type of machine. For example, the actions of a robot can be controlled by computer output, which is turned by the robot into actual physical actions.

A computer-controlled robot at work on a car assembly line

MAGNETIC STORAGE

Magnetic disks

Magnetic disks (and tapes) are made of the same materials as the video and audio tapes you have probably used at home. The surface of the disk or tape is coated with a substance which can be magnetised, and bits are recorded on the surface by a **write head** in the disk or **tape drive**.

You have probably seen **floppy disks,** which are the most common disks used with PC systems. These disks are so called because they are made of a flexible plastic material. They are enclosed in a cover for protection. Data and instructions are stored on them as a continuous stream of bits on tracks (these are a series of concentric rings on the surface of the disk – see diagram opposite).

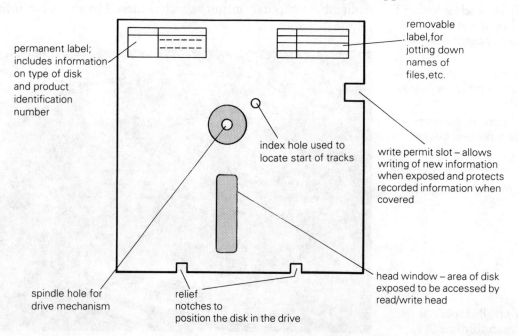

permanent label; includes information on type of disk and product identification number

removable label, for jotting down names of files, etc.

index hole used to locate start of tracks

write permit slot – allows writing of new information when exposed and protects recorded information when covered

spindle hole for drive mechanism

relief notches to position the disk in the drive

head window – area of disk exposed to be accessed by read/write head

Two sizes of floppy disk: (above) 5$\frac{1}{4}$ inch, (below) 3$\frac{1}{2}$ inch, front and back; the smaller disk is becoming more common

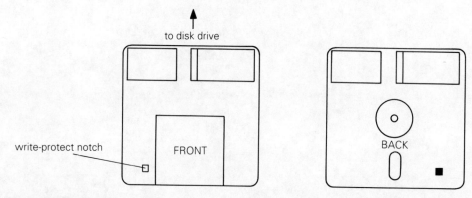

to disk drive

write-protect notch

FRONT

BACK

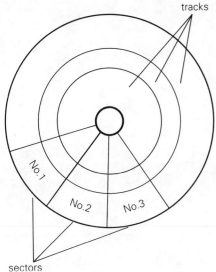

Tracks and sectors on a floppy disk

Remember that the amount of data is measured in bytes, and that one byte represents one character.

The components of a disk pack

Disks are available in a variety of sizes and **capacities** (i.e. the amount of data they can store). Capacities are measured in bytes and vary tremendously – some disks can store millions of bytes of data! All the time, new disks are being developed with larger and larger capacities.

Some of the disks that are used with large computer systems are like several 'rigid floppies' built into one unit, giving lots of surface on which to store data. Each of the surfaces is known as a **platter**, and both sides of the platter can contain data. So these disks have a very large storage capacity. Read/write heads (each like a stylus on a record player) are positioned over and under each platter and are moved in and out so that they can be positioned over the tracks.

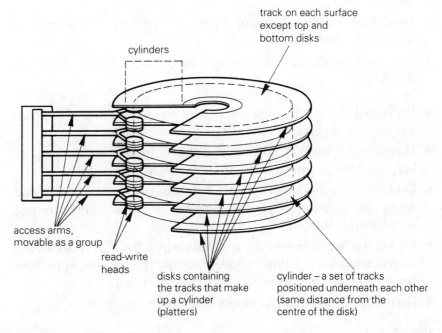

TO DO

Look at disks for sale in shops. What differences can you see between them besides the actual size?

Can the more expensive ones store more data? Is there any guarantee on them?

If possible get hold of an old floppy disk and remove the outer protection so that you can have a look at the disk itself.

Find out what type of disk you will be using, and what its capacity is.

Disks can have different numbers of tracks on them. Most floppy disks have either 40 or 80 tracks. The actual packing of the bits on each track can vary too, and these two factors combined lead to disks of different **densities**. Finally disks can be either **single-sided** or **double-sided**, depending on whether they can hold data on one or both sides.

The care of disks

All the applications software you will use, as well as the operating systems software, will come on disks. Any data or information that you produce using this software will also need to be kept on disks. So

If you are going to use a new disk in a disk drive, you need to know which type of disk you can use and how to prepare or **format** it for use.

you must understand how to care for your disks properly. The disks that you will use are much tougher than the early disks, but you still need to take care when handling and storing them. Stick to the following rules:

- *Don't* put disks on top of a television set or expose them in any way to a magnetic field, as this can 'garble' the information on them.
- *Don't* get dust or dirt on the surfaces, as this can also damage the disk; as they can contain large amounts of data the disk surface is very sensitive to even minute particles of dust.
- *Don't* put them in your pocket where they can get bent or cracked.
- *Don't* keep them in the bottom of a bag where they can get dusty.
- *Don't* let your fingers touch the surface, as they can leave grease and bits of dirt.
- *Don't* write on the labels with a pen with a hard point, as this can damage the surface.
- *Don't* expose the disks to strong sunlight or to very high or low temperatures.

- *Do* keep disks in a dry dust-free place – if you are going to build up a collection of disks, buy a disk box to keep them in.
- *Do* make sure that you label all your disks carefully, so that you can keep track of the information and software you have got.
- *Do* keep your disks in a safe place; it is easy to mislay them, and when you start to buy your own software you will discover just how valuable they are!
- *Do* use the 'write protect' on any disks which have software stored on them, so that you don't accidentally use the disk for something else – good labelling will also help to prevent this.
- *Do* use felt or soft-tipped pens for writing on the labels.

Fixed disks

The disks described so far are the type of disks which can be removed from the disk drive and carried from place to place. Some disks, however, are built into the computer or a special disk drive. These are **fixed (or hard) disks**. They are used in just the same way as removable disks, but tend to be used for storing programs or for data which has to be permanently available. (Like account details for an on-line bank cash dispenser system – the 'holes in the wall'.) Many PCs in offices have hard disks on which are kept all the regularly used programs.

Magnetic tapes

Magnetic tape works just like the tapes used in cassette players. Some home computers in fact use cassettes as extra storage. In commercial environments tapes are now used mainly to make backup copies of data held on disks – just in case anything goes wrong! **Tape streamers** are devices sometimes used for producing backups of data on to tape.

Some of these tapes are on large reels, while the more modern ones are in sealed units or cartridges – these have a much higher capacity. These cartridges can be stacked so that they will automatically fall into place when required – just like records used to be stacked on a record player. In some computer centres this job is now done by

Inside view of an automated system for storing large numbers of tape cartridges; the robotic arm is selecting a cartridge

robots, who load and unload cartridges as they are required. The reason why tapes and cartridges are used mainly for backups is that information on them can only be read **serially**. That is, it takes longer to find a piece of data than with a disk which can be read **randomly**.

serial order   random order

With **serial access**, data is read one piece after another in physical order. You could say that the players on the left will leave the field in serial order.

With **random access** data can be read in any order at all. The players on the right will go in random order.

There are several other types of magnetic storage but the use of these is limited. **Magnetic card**, for example – as used on cash cards – used to be more common in small office systems. '**Solid-state disks**' are not actual revolving disks; instead, the data is stored on chips, which appear to the processor as a disk. Access is much faster than with revolving disks.

As with input and output devices, the main problem with storage equipment concerns their mechanical parts. With disks and tape the speeds of transfer of information depend on the speed with which the read/write heads can operate and the disks can turn or the tapes wind on. For this reason the main developments in storage technology are in finding ways to reduce **access times** (how long it takes to get hold of a piece of information) and in increasing the capacities of the disks and tapes used.

OPTICAL STORAGE

This uses a laser beam to create permanent changes on the surface of a card or disk in such a way that the pattern can be read off as changes in light reflected from the surface. They have several advantages over magnetic storage:

- Optical disks have a much bigger storage capacity – 10 to 100 times greater than floppy disks.
- Optically stored data is hard to erase.
- Optical disks are easy to copy.
- Magnetic signals get weaker with age, optical ones don't.

The only disadvantages are that:

- Most optical disks are still what are called worm disks. This means 'write once read many' – in other words, once the information has been 'burnt' on to the disk you can't then write anything else on and reuse it. Reusable optical disks are starting to become available, however.
- There can be more errors made in reading an optical disk, so the error checking has to be better.
- They are still relatively expensive.

You may have come across the type of optical storage called **CD ROM** – probably you will associate it with compact disks used for music. These disks are also used with computers and have a high storage capacity. For example, the ECCTIS CD **ROM** holds details of 80 000 courses available at colleges all over the British Isles, and these details still occupy only one quarter of the disk!

TO DO

See if you can find any examples of the use of CD ROMs in your college, school or workplace. Try the careers office and have a look at the ECCTIS database, or try your library.

Lasercards are small plastic cards, like credit cards, which can each hold about 5 megabytes of information. That is about the same as 2500 pages of A4 paper! These cards could be used for holding medical information or for 'paperback books'!

A **gigadisk** can hold up to 4 gigabytes of information on a 14 inch disk. By comparison, the human brain can hold 1000 gigabits in about 4 cubic inches.

Remember you need 8 bits to store one character of data, and that a gigabit is 10^9 (a thousand million) bits.

You should now be able to:

☐ understand the need for auxiliary storage, the different types of storage available and the reasons why certain types are used for certain jobs

☐ understand the difference between serial and random access

☐ know which disks you need to use on the machine you will be working on.

5 · MOVING DATA AROUND: COMMUNICATIONS

The movement of data from one computer system to another is known as **data communications**. In many companies the trend has been away from using a single large computer, doing all the company's work (a **centralised** computer system), to several smaller machines connected together, each being used for different tasks (a **distributed** system).

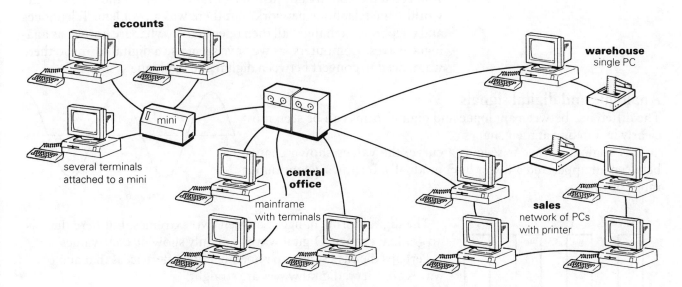

accounts

several terminals attached to a mini

mini

central office

mainframe with terminals

warehouse
single PC

sales
network of PCs with printer

A distributed computer system, showing a wide variety of sizes and arrangements of computers

In many of the old computer systems one central processor was linked to a series of **terminals** (each with a screen and a keyboard') which were used for inputting data, and one or more printers for output.

These terminals had no 'brains' or processors of their own. They simply changed human input into computer-understandable form and passed it on to the 'big machine'. These terminals were known as **dumb terminals**.

Intelligent terminals, on the other hand, have some processing power or **intelligence** themselves and can carry out the checking of input and some of the smaller jobs like word processing (see Chapter 7) without having to talk to a central processor at all. They were introduced by companies who needed their expensive central processor for processing large amounts of data and didn't want it 'clogged up' with little jobs.

This was really the point at which the **personal computer** became popular – a small machine with its own processing capacity and memory.

When you are first learning about computer systems, you will probably use what is called a **stand alone** system. This is just what was described on pages 8 to 10 – a processor, VDU and keyboard, with extra storage being provided on either floppy or hard disks and usually with a printer attached for hard copy.

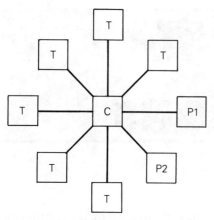

A centralised computer system: several terminal (T) and two printers (P1 and P2) connected to a central processor (C)

NETWORKS

An arrangement of computers and the peripheral devices attached to them is known as a **computer network**.

If the network covers a small area, such as a classroom or office block or a single factory site, it is known as a **local area network** – LAN for short. If it covers a greater area (for example, it might link various sites across the country or even across the world – banking networks extend worldwide) it is known as a **wide area network** or WAN.

At first, most networks were LANS – all the terminals and the main processor were situated within the same building or group of buildings. This was all that could be done to start with, as there was no way of running wires from, say, a company headquarters to all its branches across the country, to connect up **remote terminals** to the main processor.

So what could be done? The answer lay in the existing wires that connected a company not just to its branches but to the whole of the world – the telephone network. But there was a problem. Telephones and telephone exchanges all then operated on what are known as **analogue** waves. Computers, as we have seen, use a **digital** form. So there was a need to convert between digital and analogue systems.

Analogue and digital signals

The difference between analogue and digital forms can be seen most clearly by looking at their shapes.

This analogue wave is seen as a curve: the values shown change between an upper and a lower limit gradually. It shows a **continuous** range of values.

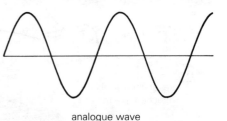

analogue wave

digital form

The digital form changes between two extremes, but here there is no gradual change. Digital waves can only show **discrete** values.

Perhaps the easiest way to remember the difference is that analogue waves are curvy, digital waves are straight.

One example of an analogue signal being converted into a digital signal for use by a computer is in the use of a temperature sensor in the control of a chemical process (pp. 28–9). The temperature curve of the chemicals in the reactor is a smooth one; the sensor changes the analogue temperature signal into a digital signal, which it sends to the control system.

If we want to send data from one computer down an analogue telephone line to another computer we need to have a converter at either end, and we would also need a piece of equipment known as a **modem** (modulator/demodulator) to establish the communication link at both ends – see diagram opposite).

GATEWAYS

With lots of different companies making communications equipment and developing it in their own way, there are now available many different types of hardware and software. Sometimes a company may

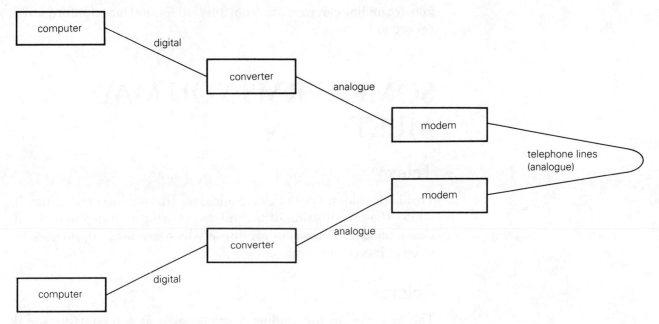

The equipment needed to send messages from one computer to another along telephone lines

want, say, to link up its head office, using one manufacturer's equipment, to a branch of the company which uses different equipment. It may not be possible to send the data directly between the two systems without first passing it through a **gateway**. The gateway is simply a piece of equipment which translates data from one form of signal to another. It is not the same as the converter in the previous diagram as the signals coming in and going out of the gateway are both digital. It simply arranges the data in a different way – rather like reducing several lanes of traffic travelling in the same direction down to a single lane.

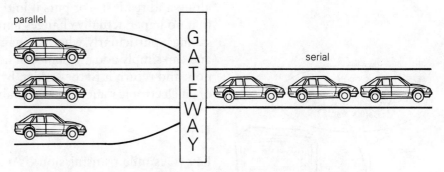

NEW DEVELOPMENTS IN COMMUNICATIONS

Today it is becoming easier to send data over the telephone network, because more of the network is now based on the use of digital equipment and signals. **Fibre optic cables** are replacing the old wires, and they are capable of transferring digital messages as light waves at a very great speed.

A company that is sending out a lot of data on a regular basis via the telephone network may well arrange for its own special links to be put in, so that the users do not have problems of sharing the network with everyone else. These links are usually described in terms of the amount of data which can be sent down them. For instance, a

kilostream line can transmit from 2400 to 64 000 bits of information per second.

SOME TERMS YOU MAY MEET

Telex

This is the oldest type of electronic data transmission technique. It allows the transmission of text messages using a limited number of characters (text messages are those which are made up mainly of words). It is rather slow.

Teletex

This is a system for sending text messages at a reasonable speed according to international standards and recommendations. It is simply a faster and improved version of Telex.

Electronic mail

This term is used to describe the sending of text messages over a network which can be large or small – i.e. within an office or across the world. You type your letter or note, you put on it the name and address of a mail box and transmit (send) the message off. At the destination the message is collected and put into the mail box until someone comes along and reads it – or puts it in the bin (deletes it)! The advantage is that no paper actually changes hands and there are considerable time savings, particularly where managers can type in their own messages and can simply add a sentence or acknowledgement to the bottom of a note and return it to the sender. British Telecom's Gold is an example of an electronic mail service available over a wide area.

Now to open my post. I wonder what Mr Banks wants?. . .

Mr Jones Mail
1. from Mr Banks
2. from................
3. ....
4. ....

Fax

Fax (facsimile transmission) is a special form of data transmission originally invented to send pictures over telecommunications lines. A picture or document is 'scanned in' and an image produced as a series of bits, which can then be sent down the telephone lines. Fax is becoming increasingly popular as it is much faster than traditional mail systems. It becomes invaluable when there is a postal strike!

Viewdata

This is a type of videotext system based on the use of the telephone lines. An example is British Telecom's Prestel service. For this a special piece of hardware has to be linked to a screen and the telephone lines. When the user requests a piece of information a page of data is sent down the telephone line. It is also possible to send information back to the remote computer on which the information is stored by using either a special videotext keyboard or a normal one. So, for example, you can use it to order goods or services from a company or use a home banking service such as that run by the Bank of Scotland. Prestel was meant to provide armchair shopping but it has tended to be used as an information source by businesses rather than by individuals in their own homes. Over the years it has widened its facilities so that now a simple viewdata set can provide many of the needs of, for example, travel agents.

It is now possible to provide access to private information systems, the access being restricted by the use of passwords, and to other public data communications services such as Telex and electronic mail.

Campus 2000 is the Prestel and Telecom Gold service for education, and provides such services as electronic mail, database access and conferencing for its users.

Broadcast services

As well as being able to use telephone lines to transmit data around the country and the world it is also possible to use **broadcast** techniques, particularly for data which is for the use of everyone. One example of this, known as Teletext, is the BBC's Ceefax service. The pictures on an ordinary television screen are made up of a series of lines, and the Ceefax service simply uses some of the spare lines to send information which can be picked up by special receivers. Information is not sent in response to the user's demand, so you have to wait for the required pages to be broadcast.

This service was intended for the use of companies at times when there was not much demand for personal viewing. But the reverse happened and the system is now widely used by households all over the country – usually at peak viewing times!

The above are just some of the computer network services available. There are many others, from those where you can pick up new programs for your computer (usually games) to the serious networks used by universities for exchanging research data or by libraries for providing information on local services to the public.

TO DO (1)

Find out how much it would cost and how long it would take to send

- a single-page document such as a letter, and
- a twenty-page report

by as many different electronic methods as you can find. Compare these with the cost and time taken to send them by post.

TO DO (2)

Ask at work or in your college/school office when they use each of the different methods for transferring data – remember they may not have them all available.

Find out if you can use the Campus 2000 system in your school or local college.

You should now be able to:

☐ understand the wide range of electronic communication methods available

☐ understand the type of data you would send or receive using each

☐ understand some of the terms in describing data communication techniques.

On its own, computer hardware – the keyboard, the VDU and the central processor – can do nothing. It needs instructions to make it work. These instructions are the **software**. However clever and sophisticated the various pieces of hardware are, they still need software to make them work.

Computers themselves are not clever! They are only able to do exactly what they are told to do. So it is the skill of the person writing the software which enables users to make the most of all the technology available today.

SYSTEMS SOFTWARE

In an office without computers the staff have to do certain routine jobs: filing, sending and opening the post, moving documents from place to place, getting rid of old information, reorganising the workspace and so forth. In just the same way, there are routine tasks which have to be done to allow computer systems to work efficiently.

Housekeeping in the office

These tasks are carried out by the computer following the instructions it has been given. The software written to perform these basic routine tasks is called **systems software**, as it is concerned with **running the system**, or making it work.

Examples of systems software are the instructions needed to start the computer system working, and the software that allows the main processor to talk to peripheral devices, to send or receive messages and to organise and prepare disks for use. Sometimes systems software is divided up into **operating systems** and **communications software**.

Operating systems are one example of systems software. They come either built into a PC on a ROM chip, or as a separate piece of software. The operating system does just what the name suggests: it allows you to operate or use the machine. There is usually little choice of which operating system you can use on your machine as the actual design of the processor affects this. For the PC the most common operating systems are MS-DOS and PC DOS, and more recently Unix.

Communications software, very simply, is the programs written to allow computers to 'talk' to one another. For example, when computers are linked together in a network sharing data, something needs to control just which machine has access to the data at any given time. Without this control, all sorts of problems could result!

The set of instructions written to allow networking of computers is one example of **communications software.**

TO DO

Find out which operating system your computer uses and where it is located. There are several possibilities:

● It may be built into the processor as 'firmware', so that as soon as you switch on the machine the commands are available and a **prompt** of some sort appears on the screen to show you that the computer is waiting for an instruction from you.

● It may be stored on a hard disk within the machine itself. If so, then someone must have installed the operating system software for you already and copied it on to the hard disk ready for use. Again, a prompt appears when the machine is ready for use.

● The operating system comes on a floppy disk, which you have to put into the disk drive of your computer, and then follow any instructions that appear on the screen.

Manuals

If you buy any piece of hardware or software, then along with it you should get a **manual** or **user's guide**. These are your instructions to show you how to get the computer to perform the jobs you want it to do. Always read your manuals carefully before doing anything with the software and keep them in a safe place where you can easily refer to them. No one can remember everything, and anyone who uses a computer needs to be able to look things up.

Using systems software

Files and filenames

At this point you need to make sure you understand the idea of a suite or collection of programs. DOS is a collection of lots of different programs, each of which contains the instructions for the computer to perform one task. Each of these programs will have been given a name by the person who wrote it, so that when you want to use that particular set of instructions you can tell the computer to find and carry them out. The print-out shows part of a list of the different programs that can be found on a DOS disk.

file name	extension	size of file in bytes	date and time last altered	
EMM	SYS	21355	12-12-90	9:00a
SMARTDRV	SYS	10354	05-09-90	9:00a
APPEND	EXE	11154	10-04-89	9:00a
ASSIGN	COM	5753	10-04-89	9:00a
ATTRIB	EXE	18263	10-04-89	9:00a
BACKUP	COM	36958	10-06-89	9:00a
CHKDSK	COM	17755	10-06-89	9:00a
COMP	COM	9459	10-04-89	9:00a
DEBUG	COM	21622	10-04-89	9:00a

Look carefully at the way the programs are labelled in the print-out. Each of the programs is known by a **filename**, just as if it were stored in a folder in a filing cabinet, and it is stored in a particular place on the disk. Filenames cannot be made up in any old way. There are certain rules which must be kept to when choosing them.

TO DO

Find out the rules which apply to filenames with your operating system.

Most filenames also have what is called an **extension** to the filename, which is generally three characters long. This indicates what type of information is stored in that file. Notice that when you write them down, the filename should be separated from the extension by a full stop.

TO DO

Look at the list in the print-out and see how many different extensions you can see.

The extensions are used generally mean different things. Some of the most common ones are as follows:

- COM – contains a set of commands for the computer to follow
- EXE – contains a set of executable commands
- SYS – contains commands which are used by the computer to set the system up ready for use
- DAT – contains data (not instructions).

Finally on filenames – it is always a good idea to give sensible names to the files you make. All too often people use something that gives them no idea of a file's contents when they look at a list of their files, even as little as a week after they last used them. So be careful and use sensible names which tell you as much as possible about the contents of the file. For example, a file containing information on addresses of customers might be called CUSTADD.DAT.

TO DO

Using the rules given above see if you can make up filenames with extensions for the following types of file:

- a file containing a letter written to sales representatives
- a file containing a set of instructions to the computer to format or prepare a new disk
- a file containing data on employees
- a file containing instructions to the computer on how to communicate with a printer.

Housekeeping

Most people use an operating system to get their computer started and to 'load' another piece of software. Other systems software is usually available with the operating system software and these programs are used for various different jobs, including **housekeeping**. Housekeeping is, as the name suggests, concerned with organising and keeping your disks in a tidy and efficient manner. Practise all the commands explained in this section until you can use them all the time without having to keep looking them up in a manual.

The most useful 'housekeeping' programs are described below.

- FORMAT   This program is used to prepare floppy disks for use. This preparation of a disk is called **formatting**. It is rather like clearing out or organising an empty filing cabinet ready for use.

  Just as you would check through the cabinet looking for any damaged dividers and labelling the different parts of the cabinet ready for use, so the computer following the commands given in the FORMAT program of the operating system prepares a new or old disk for use.

- DIRECTORY   We frequently need to be able to see what files there are on a disk. On page 50 there is a diagram showing a list of DOS files: this list was obtained using the DIRECTORY program.

- COPY   The COPY program is used to copy files from one disk to another. It is useful to be able to do this when we need to send someone a disk with certain of our data files on it or to make a backup copy (see page 75) of them on a separate disk for safe keeping.

Never copy any files unless you have permission to do so. People sometimes copy software borrowed from their friends or work colleagues. This stops the producers of the software from selling their products, and it is in fact a criminal offence.

An **operating system** is the set of instructions which allow a human to use the machinery and to carry out the routine tasks needed to 'run' the system.

- DELETE   Often after a while your files may get out of date and you may need to get rid of some to save space on the disk. It's as if you had a filing cabinet full of information on suppliers or customers, and needed to clear out all the old files every year and perhaps save them for a further twelve months before throwing them away (**archiving**). You may decide to take the same approach with the files on your disk, but while you are learning you will probably find that you need to have a sort-out fairly often!

There are lots of other systems software programs available which you will gradually pick up as you want to do more with your computer. For the work that you will cover in this book, however, the ones described above are sufficient.

APPLICATIONS SOFTWARE

You have already seen that there are lots of different ways in which computers can be used. It follows that there must be lots of different sets of instructions which can be used to make the computers perform all these different jobs or **applications**. This is what **applications software** is. For example, one piece of applications software might be made up of the instructions necessary to get a computer to prepare, add and find records from a list of names and addresses.

Below are details of some of the most commonly used types of applications software. Some of these are dealt with in more detail in Chapters 7 to 10 of this book.

Word processing

A computer **program** is a set of instructions designed to allow the computer to perform a particular job.

This is probably the most commonly used type of applications program. As the name suggests, it allows a user to input words and arrange them as they wish, move them around, delete bits and insert new sections. The output can be shown on the screen or sent to a printer. This book has been written using a very simple word processing package. It has been a lot easier to correct mistakes than if every page had had to be retyped each time I made a slip!

Some computers are **dedicated** word processors – that is, word processing is the only job they can do. An example is the Amstrad PCW. Others have a word processor built in as firmware, such as the program EDWORD on some BBC machines. Common word processing programs used in the business world include WordPerfect, DisplayWrite and WordStar.

Word processing packages (this term is often used instead of 'program' to indicate that more than one program is involved) are in many ways the easiest for people to see the benefits of. There are problems, however. Some managers say they won't use one because they aren't typists! Other people are put off because they cannot type quickly. Often it doesn't matter that you are not a fast typist: just copying something in is very different from thinking about what you want to say at the same time as you are typing. I can only use two fingers on each hand and get up to only about twenty words per minute, but this doesn't matter!

Word processing is described in more detail in Chapter 7.

Make a list of things for which you could use a word processor: for example, letter writing, producing a curriculum vitae, writing essays, reports and projects.

Look again at the definition of a program on page 52. You can see that a program performs *one* task. Often it is necessary to combine several tasks together to make one application (like using several building blocks to make one structure). The best programs are the ones that are not too long or complicated. This is why manufacturers usually sell software **packages** – groups of programs necessary to perform one application. For example, a word processing package might include a program for editing the text, one for printing out, one for helping the user, and so on.

Spreadsheets and accounting packages

One of the first commercial uses of computers was in the accounts departments of companies, for it is there that thousands of routine calculations are done – just the sort of thing for which computers are much better than humans. At first separate programs were written for each individual company, but gradually packages of programs dealing with all the different accounting jobs were built up. There are now many of these for sale including Lotus (a general-purpose spreadsheet package), Sage and Pegasus. These accounting software packages have been of great benefit, particularly to the smaller businesses who could not afford to have programs written just for themselves.

Sometimes a company will go out and buy a piece of packaged software **off the shelf**. Often this will not quite meet the needs of the company, so they may have to have it 'tailored' or **customised** to suit them. If there really isn't anything that fits the company's needs or which can be customised, then they may get someone to write a set of programs just for them – this is **bespoke** software.

A spreadsheet is just a method of showing information. It can be compiled either manually or by computer. Spreadsheets were around long before computers! See Chapter 9 for more information on these.

Stock control

As you have already seen, many supermarkets and shops use computer systems. The automated control of stock is one of the jobs for which these systems are most commonly used. If a company can control its stock levels accurately it can save a great deal of money: the need for warehousing is reduced, surplus stock is not wasted, and so on. IBM, for example, do not carry stocks of computers at all – they are actually manufactured as and when the customer asks for them. The same idea is just taking off with car manufacturers in the USA – you go to a salesroom and order your car giving details of colour, engine size and so forth, and the car is then made to order.

Payroll

This is another of those jobs where it is easy for the person doing the

A computer cannot make a mistake! The only mistakes are human ones – either someone has fed in the wrong input, or the person who wrote the program has given the compuger the wrong instructions. Remember that when you get the next bill with mistakes in it!

job to make mistakes. Large companies and local authorities were the first to use computers for payrolls because of the obvious savings in time that could be made. Just imagine how much easier it is to tell a computer to add, say, another 8 per cent to everyone's wages when a pay rise is awarded than for a person to calculate the increase for each of perhaps a thousand employees! And because computers themselves cannot make mistakes, a lot of queries over pay should also be avoided.

TO DO

If you receive a payslip, or can look at someone else's, work out whether the payslip is produced by a computer. If so, see if you can tell what calculations have been done with which pieces of data.

Information retrieval

You have probably seen the information screens used in travel agents' offices. But there are lots of other possible uses of software designed for storing and retrieving information. In the home such a system might be used for keeping information on people's birthdays, for recipes, for a hobby such as stamp collecting or for any type of cataloguing. In businesses information on customers and suppliers, on staff and on equipment can all be kept. The growth in information retrieval systems is probably one of the most significant recent developments in the use of computers.

Many of the information retrieval systems in use are based on **database management systems**. These are sets of programs designed to help people to enter, store and retrieve information. This type of software is described more fully in Chapter 8 of this book.

CAD, CAG and CAM

These three application areas – computer-aided design, computer-aided graphics (p. 119) and computer-aided manufacture respectively – really speak for themselves. They have revolutionised the ways in which many people work. Software has been developed specifically for these different tasks. For the first two tasks, several packages are available for the personal computer, and these can be used for a whole range of purposes. A graphics package used to design a house could probably just as easily be used for designing an aircraft wing or a new car.

On the other hand, many of the programs for CAM have to be specially written for each particular use. For example, a piece of CAM software designed to control the operation of a machine tool cutting sheets of metal probably wouldn't be appropriate in the textile industry for machines cutting material. Most CAM software is therefore customised or bespoke.

CAL – computer-assisted learning

In this type of software the computer takes on the role of a teacher or tutor. There are various types of CAL on the market: programs developed to help slow learners, spelling and maths programs, programs to teach children about the environment or a foreign language, and so on. Some of the programs are simple and repetitive. Some actually learn about the person using the program, so that they can either ask steadily harder questions or keep going back to something the user has not understood.

The demand for CAL packages is growing very fast, and so is the number of programs on the market. In the commercial world they can be used in the training of staff in a new product. Suppose, for example, a building society decides to introduce a new type of savings account. Instead of getting all the branch staff into the head office for training sessions (very expensive!) a program might be written which explains the new account and which can be copied and sent to every branch. This can be much cheaper, particularly where a lot of employees need training; besides, the package is always there for staff to refer to if they forget something – a tutor wouldn't be. Unfortunately, well-written CAL software takes a long time to produce, and can be very expensive.

TO DO

Find out the names and the uses of the different types of applications software which you will be able to use.

DEVELOPING A COMPUTER PROGRAM

A computer program is just a list of instructions for the computer to follow to do a job. So it must be easy to write one! Is that what you think?

TO DO

Write a set of instructions explaining exactly how to tie a tie, or to make a cup of tea. Try them out on a friend – don't interrupt to help them or show them how to do it. How did they get on?

Writing programs isn't quite that simple! There are several stages involved, and the first and hardest part is in making sure that you know *exactly* what needs to be done by the computer.

TO DO

Make a list of things that you have to do at home, work or school which you think a computer could do for you. Remember what sort of tasks computers are best at. Choose one of these jobs and write out a set of instructions which you would need to give to the computer to do the job.

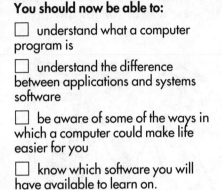

You should now be able to:

☐ understand what a computer program is

☐ understand the difference between applications and systems software

☐ be aware of some of the ways in which a computer could make life easier for you

☐ know which software you will have available to learn on.

Take hold of the tie in your right hand . . . . .

Problem analysis

This is the name given to the job of finding out what needs to be done. A person who carries out this job is called a **systems analyst**. The work is quite skilled because it may involve talking to people who have never used a computer and who don't want to. Also people do certain jobs 'automatically', without really thinking what they are doing. The analyst must be able to pick up all these things, so needs to be good at listening and communicating. Analysts also have to know just what computer systems are capable of, and be able to decide whether using a computer really is the best way of solving any problems they have found.

The drawing shows a simple problem that occurs in most dentists' surgeries. A patient wants to book an appointment to visit her own dentist. The receptionist has to find out certain information and then provide the patient with an appointment. The problem with this booking system is the amount of time the receptionist has to spend finding the ideal appointment while trying to cope with other patients arriving, the phone ringing and so on.

A systems analyst would try to find out the way the job is done and the information which is input to the system and output from it.

In our example the job is done by the receptionist asking questions, then flicking back and forth through a diary to find a free appointment, and checking this with the patient. If the time is convenient he will book it in. If not, then the search for a suitable slot has to be repeated until a suitable time is found. Then the appointment is made and entered into the diary and on to a card for the patient. The input data will be:

> the patient's name
> the times and days the patient can be available
> spare appointment slots
> the dentist's name
> whether the appointment is urgent or routine
> how long an appointment is required.

The output data is:

> the date and time of the appointment.

When the analyst has got all the information needed, it must all be written down and checked with the person who is going to pay for the system and use it. This is called the **specification**. It will be written in English, so that the dentists themselves can understand it.

Once this has been agreed the analyst moves on to 'design a solution' to the problem. This solution would have to take into account how much the dentists have to spend on a system, whether they already have a computer which just needs a new piece of software to do this job, how quickly the job needs doing, how many people will need to be able to use the system, how much training they will need and so on. Only after this has been done will the programming begin.

The **programmer's** job is to take the specification and to design, translate (or code) the program(s) required and to test them and get rid of any errors. All the way through the analyst will be involved, making sure that the system does what the specification says it will do and that the people who are going to use it are properly trained and have well-written instructions or documentation to go with the programs.

The actual design of the program is where every little step which the computer needs to perform is worked out and put into a logical order. All of this will be done in English, or a special reduced form of English known as **structured English** or **pseudocode**. Only when this has been done will coding take place. **Coding** is the translation of English instructions into a computer-understandable language. Increasingly this is being done by computers themselves, because it is a very 'routine job'.

Once the programs have been coded they are then tested and any errors removed. The users are then introduced to the new system and shown how to make the best use of it, with the help of manuals provided by the analyst and programmer. When the program or **suite** of programs has been set up and is working the system is then what is known as **live** – it is actually being used to do the job.

Sometimes all the jobs described above are done by one person who would then be called an **analyst programmer** – this is usually the case where small PC-based systems are involved. A big job such as an accounting system for a large company will require many analysts and programmers, who will work in teams on parts of the whole system. This will ensure that the work is completed reasonably quickly.

A few people have had bad experiences with computers, usually as a result of either being sold the wrong hardware or (more commonly) having to use badly designed software – it doesn't do what they want it to do. Or they may not have been trained properly in how to use the system. Often manuals are written badly, in language which is difficult for people who are not experts to understand. But problems like these should not occur at all. They only happen when the stages outlined above have not been carried out thoroughly.

PROGRAMMING LANGUAGES

Just as there are lots of different languages that people speak, there are many different programming languages that computers can understand.

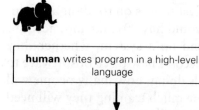

human writes program in a high-level language

↓

human gets computer to compile (translate) this into machine code

↓

computer can understand and follow the low-level machine code

The early computers were not very clever, and the language which was used to give them instructions had to be very easy for the machine to understand. This type of language is called **machine code** and it is what is known as a **low-level language** – that is, computers find it very simple to understand. There are different types of machine code, and the type to be used with any computer depends on the actual hardware or the way the computer was built.

Unfortunately, writing programs in machine code is a tedious, slow and boring business. So a lot of development went into producing other languages which were easier for humans to understand but which could then be translated into machine code for computers to understand. These are known as **high-level languages**. In other words, the process of communicating with the machine became a two-level process. The pieces of software that translate the higher-level programming languages into machine code are called compilers.

Unlike the low-level programming languages, high-level languages can be used on a variety of machines providing a compiler is used that translates in a way that the machine used can understand. Examples of high-level languages are COBOL and BASIC (see below). The advantages of high-level languages are:

- they can be designed to cater for different user environments (scientific, process control, commercial, for instance)
- programs can be used on more than one type of machine
- programming is easier, therefore faster and less expensive
- programming can become something more and more people can do for themselves.

All the time people are writing new programming languages, with the aim of making them closer and closer to English and therefore easier and easier to use. The sooner we can just talk to the computer and tell it what to do, the sooner everyone will feel at ease using one!

Some common languages and their uses

COBOL
This stands for COmmon Business-Oriented Language. It was designed to be used in commercial environments, where large amounts of data have to be processed – for example, in banking and finance, accounting and personnel systems. It is a good language for producing reports and dealing with large amounts of input, but it is not good for what are known as 'interactive programs' (i.e. those where there is communication between the user and the computer, such as database management programs and word processing programs). Currently there are more programs around written in COBOL than in any other language.

BASIC
This – Beginner's All-purpose Symbolic Instruction Code – is probably still the most popular programming language for people to use to learn the art of programming. It is also one which if badly taught can allow people to get into very bad programming habits! It is available on many of the home computers as firmware – built into the machine when it was manufactured.

PASCAL

This language, named after the famous seventeenth-century French mathematician Blaise Pascal by its inventor, Nicholas Wirth, is often used along with FORTRAN for scientific applications. It has become used increasingly in the teaching of programming because it forces good habits on programmers!

C

This is increasingly taking over from PASCAL and COBOL as the most widely used language for commercial programming.

PROLOG

PROLOG is a relatively new language which, along with LISP, is used with information retrieval and expert systems packages.

Fourth-generation languages (4GLs)

These languages are supposed to be the nearest to English that are available at the moment, and are more suited to producing interactive programs. There are lots of different ones around and many are 'tied' to particular pieces of packaged software, in particular what are known as database packages. One example is INFOMIX. The most widely used 4GL is SQL (Structured Query Language), which is available with such database packages as Oracle and dbase4. A 4GL should allow users to write their own programs, rather than paying computer specialists to do the job!

Very few people actually need to be able to write programs to use a computer effectively. This is because there is now such a large range of packaged software available 'off the shelf' that not many users need to write their own. It is unfortunate that many people think that programming is the most important job to do with computers – it isn't! The most useful people are those who understand enough about computers, and about information technology in general, to be able to see how and where it can be used to the best advantage. Programming itself is becoming easier for anyone to do. It will soon be done by the machines themselves!

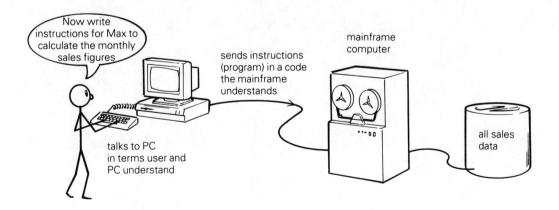

One computer can now be used to produce programs for another

SECURITY

Taking care of your disks and making backup copies are simple precautions which everyone can take to keep their software and data secure. Everyone also needs to be aware of the problems of illegally copying other software (anything which you have not bought or which is not copyright-free). There is some software around which is freely available, and some of the computer magazines come with free sample disks that can be used legally.

Finally, remember that disks can pick up what are known as **viruses** – programs which have been written to 'contaminate' or interfere with people's disks or machines. It is easy to prevent getting these on to your own disks: just never lend them to other people or use any copied software from others. If in doubt, always ask for advice.

The Data Protection Act

This Act was brought in to prevent companies from storing all sorts of information on people without them being aware of it. Anyone storing computerised information on other people has to declare to the **Data Protection Office** the information they keep, and they have to be **registered** to do so. This Act will not have any importance for the casual computer user, but if you are intending to keep information for any business purpose then you should find out more about it. Information is obtainable from the Data Protection Registrar, Springfield House, Water Lane, Wilmslow, Cheshire SK9 5AX.

You should now be able to:

☐ understand the main stages involved in writing a computer program

☐ understand that instructions must be very simple for computers to understand

☐ be familiar with the names of the main programming languages and what they are used for.

Part II

GETTING TO KNOW YOUR COMPUTER SYSTEM

7 · WORD PROCESSING

Probably the most widely used type of computer applications software around at the moment is the word processor. In simple terms, its name says exactly what it can do – process words. In many offices the use of word processing software has made the typewriter redundant, and now a wide variety of retraining courses is available for typists to update their skills.

But not only typists use word processing programs. They are one of the most useful kinds of programs available. Many different people use them: students producing homework, writers producing books and articles, and business people producing reports.

WHAT CAN YOU USE THEM FOR?

Word processing software can be used to enter, store, retrieve, edit and print data.

The whole idea of word processors was a huge step forward in the use of computers, because it represented a real change in their use from dealing with numbers to dealing with words. As many people find words easier to cope with than numbers, the development of word processing software led to an increase in the use of computers. Suddenly people realised you didn't have to be a whizz mathematician to use them!

This is why word processors are one of the easiest pieces of software for computer beginners to choose. The only disadvantage is that if you cannot type fast you may feel a little frustrated at first, as your brain will work more quickly than your fingers.

'Come on fingers, keep up!'

Don't despair! Unless you are a professional typist, you don't need to be able to type particularly fast, and it is amazing how you speed up as you get used to the computer.

What does a word processing program do?

When we type in a document, the word processing program holds the keyed-in information in the RAM of the computer's processor until we **save** our work.

As we **enter** the information we see the document on the monitor, and can lay it out as we want it. It is kept in the RAM as a **stream of characters**. This includes not just the letters, commas, full stops and so forth that we actually type, but extra characters which the program inserts to show where the paragraphs end, where there are blank lines or spaces, where the document starts and ends and the name we have given it.

If you save the document the stream of characters is **copied** and **written** on to the disk you have chosen, and **indexed** by the name you have given it. This means that you now have the document **stored** on a disk.

Once the document has been stored, you can **retrieve** the document from the disk at any time and **edit** or change the information in it. The document will remain on the disk for as long as you want it to, and can be changed as many times as you want.

If you **print** the document the stream of characters is copied to the printer, which then follows the instructions the program gives it to interpret the characters and print out the document.

TO DO

Think of what jobs you might use a word processing package for. Can you see how it could make life easier for you?

WHAT YOU NEED

All you need to start are the following:

hardware: keyboard
               processor
               monitor
               printer

software: operating system
             word processing package (your applications software).

There are many different word processing packages on the market today. Some are even built into processors as firmware (see page 49); for example, EDWORD is a word processor that is often built into BBC computers. Increasingly, **integrated software** is sold: this combines word processors with other applications software, such as database or spreadsheet packages (see Chapters 8 and 9), and you may find that it is ideal for your purposes. An example of an integrated package is Open Access. Of the specialist word processors the most common are WordPerfect, WordStar and DisplayWrite.

Dedicated word processors

These are computers which have been built for one purpose – word processing. They cannot be used to run other types of applications software.

TO DO

Find out which word processing package you are going to use, and where you can get a copy of the manual or an instruction book to go with it.

WHAT YOU WILL LEARN IN THIS CHAPTER

In the rest of this chapter you will be shown how to use some of the basic commands in a typical word processing package. The exercises included should enable you to get going on your own, but you will need to refer to your own manual, teacher or colleagues to check on the actual commands to use with your own word processing software.

This book will show you *what* you can do using a word processing program, rather than exactly *how* to do it. It will also indicate the advantages for you of using word processing software.

You may need help to **install** your word processing software if you are using a computer with a hard disk. You may also need help to attach and set up your printer so that it can understand the instructions sent by the word processing program when you wish to print out.

You should now be able to:

☐ explain what a word processing package can do

☐ be aware which word processing package you are going to use, and where to find the instructions you need to be able to use it.

GETTING STARTED

The first thing you will need to do is to **load** your word processing package into the memory of the machine you are going to use.

TO DO

Load your software. If you do not know how to do this, look in your manual or ask your teacher.

You are now ready to start learning some of the commands. To start off with you will only need to become familiar with the commands to:

- open a document
- edit a file
- print a file
- exit.

A word processing package can be used to enter, edit, save, retrieve and print documents.

TO DO

Look at your own word processing package's menu or manual and find the **commands** for these actions.

Naming data files

When you use a word processing package to produce a letter or memo, you need to be able to give the document a name. Most people develop their own **naming conventions**, but if you are using a computer at work then you should find out if there are any rules or **standards** in use for naming data files. For example, when writing this book I named my data files by section and page number, and I used the extension to indicate that they were part of a book. For example,

CHA21.bk

meant Chapter 2 page 1 of the book, and

CHA310.bk

meant Chapter 3 page 10 of the book.

Other names I use often consist of a person's name and date, with the extension indicating the type of document. For example,

SYL1910.mem

would be a memo written to Sylvia on 19 October.

Remember that you cannot have two files with the same name. The computer will get confused as to which one you want!

TO DO

Work out what types of document you are likely to use and see if you can devise a sensible naming system for them. Don't forget to follow the operating system rules for filenames and extensions. The examples shown above are suitable for use with the DOS operating system.

Printing a file

This is something you will want to do when you have finished your first document. To avoid disappointment, do make sure that your system includes software necessary for the printer to be able to understand the output from the word processing package you are using. This should be installed at the same time as the word processing package.

Exit

This is what you do when you have finished using the program. You must get into the habit of doing this properly, rather than just taking your disks out and switching off (or, even worse, switching off without removing the disks!) If you do not exit a program properly then problems can arise with your data – this is particularly true with database programs (see Chapter 8).

Most word processing packages start with a menu, offering choices of actions like those described above. That is, they are examples of what is known as **menu-driven software**, where your actions are limited to the options shown on the menu. The diagram shows the menu line from WordStar.

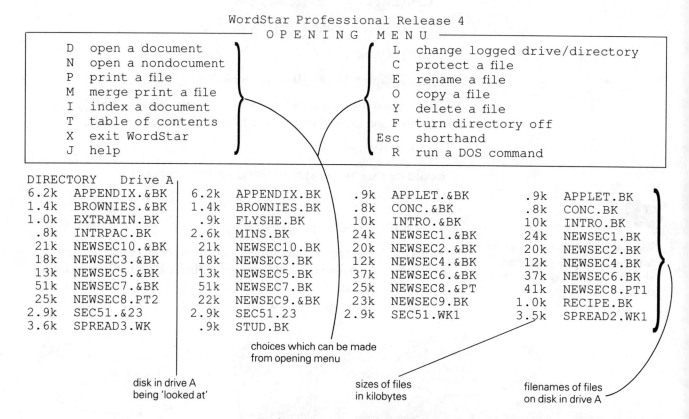

```
                  WordStar Professional Release 4
                  ──── O P E N I N G   M E N U ────

   D  open a document              L    change logged drive/directory
   N  open a nondocument           C    protect a file
   P  print a file                 E    rename a file
   M  merge print a file           O    copy a file
   I  index a document             Y    delete a file
   T  table of contents            F    turn directory off
   X  exit WordStar              Esc    shorthand
   J  help                         R    run a DOS command
```

```
DIRECTORY     Drive A
6.2k   APPENDIX.&BK      6.2k   APPENDIX.BK      .9k   APPLET.&BK       .9k   APPLET.BK
1.4k   BROWNIES.&BK      1.4k   BROWNIES.BK      .8k   CONC.&BK         .8k   CONC.BK
1.0k   EXTRAMIN.BK        .9k   FLYSHE.BK        10k   INTRO.&BK        10k   INTRO.BK
 .8k   INTRPAC.BK        2.6k   MINS.BK          24k   NEWSEC1.&BK      24k   NEWSEC1.BK
21k    NEWSEC10.&BK      21k    NEWSEC10.BK      20k   NEWSEC2.&BK      20k   NEWSEC2.BK
18k    NEWSEC3.&BK       18k    NEWSEC3.BK       12k   NEWSEC4.&BK      12k   NEWSEC4.BK
13k    NEWSEC5.&BK       13k    NEWSEC5.BK       37k   NEWSEC6.&BK      37k   NEWSEC6.BK
51k    NEWSEC7.&BK       51k    NEWSEC7.BK       25k   NEWSEC8.&PT      41k   NEWSEC8.PT1
25k    NEWSEC8.PT2       22k    NEWSEC9.&BK      23k   NEWSEC9.BK      1.0k   RECIPE.BK
2.9k   SEC51.&23        2.9k    SEC51.23        2.9k   SEC51.WK1       3.5k   SPREAD2.WK1
3.6k   SPREAD3.WK         .9k   STUD.BK
```

choices which can be made
from opening menu

disk in drive A
being 'looked at'

sizes of files
in kilobytes

filenames of files
on disk in drive A

To begin with, you are going to feel that there are an awful lot of commands and things to remember and that really it isn't worth all the bother. It is, in fact, amazing how quickly you begin to remember the commands and the saying 'practice makes perfect' is true of using any computer program!

If you are already familiar with the terms used in typing, you will find them helpful as you work on this section. If not, don't worry if you find progress is slow at the start – persevere!

WHAT HAPPENS NEXT?

When you have decided on a filename, you need to **create** a document. Then in order to type in information you need to go into what is called **edit mode**. Find out how you do this with your own word processing package.

TO DO

Create a new document file using the filename TEST.DOC.

Help!

Everybody needs help at some time when they are using a word processing package, and one way of telling whether a program is well-written is by the standard of the help available. If you find the 'help' facility easy to use and understand, the program is a good one for you. If you find it difficult or confusing then that program is not the one to use, and certainly not the one to learn on.

Frequently the key to press to get help is F1.

Status lines

At either the top or the bottom of your screen, you will find a line of information known as the **status line**. The exact information which is shown on this varies slightly from one word processing package to another, but generally the information shown includes:

- the name of the document you are working on
- the page, line and column numbers for the **cursor** position
- whether you are in **insert** or **overwrite** mode (see page 76)
- whether you are using **justification** or not (see page 74).

Here is an example of a status line:

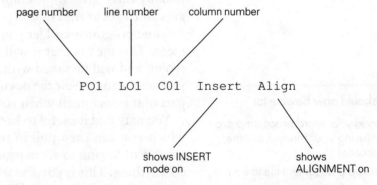

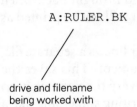

The status line is the first place you should look at if you want to check what is happening as you type.

Ruler lines

The **ruler line** is another line of information that may be shown permanently on the screen while you are working. The purpose of this line is to show you the **layout** or positioning of your work across the page. The ruler line will show the position of your **left** and **right margins** and of any Tab (**tabulation**) marks you have set. **Tabulation marks** are positions which you might set when typing in, for example, lists of names and addresses or columns of figures. Instead of having to type in the precise number of spaces all the time to get to the positions you want you can simply press the Tab key to move across the line to the correct position. Many people use Tab marks to set up the position for **indenting** paragraphs (i.e. starting the first line of each paragraph a little way in from the left-hand margin – as in this book).

The next diagram shows an example of a ruler line with the Tab positions marked by exclamation marks, the left margin with L and the right with R, together with options for the on-screen formatting of text.

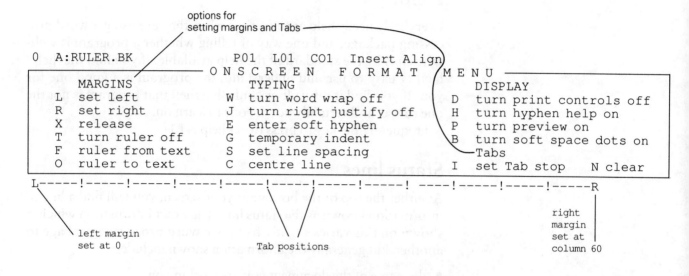

options for
setting margins and Tabs

```
0   A:RULER.BK              P01  L01  CO1  Insert Align
          ─────────────  O N S C R E E N   F O R M A T   M E N U ─────────────
    MARGINS                    TYPING                         DISPLAY
  L  set left            W  turn word wrap off        D  turn print controls off
  R  set right           J  turn right justify off    H  turn hyphen help on
  X  release             E  enter soft hyphen         P  turn preview on
  T  turn ruler off      G  temporary indent          B  turn soft space dots on
  F  ruler from text     S  set line spacing          ─Tabs
  O  ruler to text       C  centre line               I  set Tab stop    N clear
L─────!─────!─────!─────!─────!─────!─────!─────!─────! ────!─────!─────!─────R
```

left margin
set at 0

Tab positions

right
margin
set at
column 60

Setting the ruler line positions

If you do not set the ruler line before you type anything in, then the program will use the **default** line which is built into the program. If this suits you, then simply carry on. If you wish to change anything, you must find out from your manual or teacher how to do this. Usually there are simple commands which allow you to set the margins and Tabs at the column positions that you want.

Some programs will let you save the ruler line as part of the document. This means that it will stay on the screen all the time you are typing and will be saved with the document and brought back when you next want to edit the document, although it will not be printed as part of the document when you print out.

You may find it useful to keep a **standard** ruler line as a separate file, which you can then pull in to use in any document. This saves the trouble of having to set margins and so forth every time you want to do anything. This is particularly useful when writing something like a book, when you want to keep the same settings in lots of different files.

You should now be able to:

☐ load your word processing program (using your manual or other instructions)
☐ set up a document file to edit
☐ use a simple menu
☐ read the status line
☐ and set up a ruler line.

TO DO

Find out what information is shown on the status line in your package and how to set up a ruler line.

Then set up a ruler line for the file TEST.DOC, with a left margin at column 5 and a right margin at column 70.

The cursor

As when using operating system software, the cursor shows you where you are up to and where the next letter you type will appear. Often the size of the cursor is an indication of whether you are using capital letters or not – it becomes larger when the CAPS LOCK is on and smaller when it is not.

COMMON FEATURES OF WORD PROCESSORS

Wordwrap

One of the first things you notice when you start to use a word processing package is that you no longer have to stop typing when you think you are reaching the end of a line so that you can reposition yourself at the start of the next line (the 'carriage return' on typewriters). The word processor does this for you. This feature is called **wordwrap** – what you type is automatically wrapped round on to the next line once the end of the line is reached. Words are not split between two lines, as the program recognises the length of a word by the spaces it finds before and after it and calculates whether the word will fit on the end of a line or not.

TO DO

Using your file TEST.DOC, type in a really, really long sentence like the first sentence on this page, and watch what happens when you get to the end of the line.

If you find that the sentence did not wrap round on to the next line, this is because you have not got wordwrap set 'on', and you need to check your manual or ask for help to put it on. The status line may indicate whether wordwrap is on or not.

As described earlier, the document you produce will be saved as a long stream of characters. As you type them in, the letters and spaces are recorded in this stream. The program will insert into this special characters to show where the ends of lines come when you are using wordwrap. But what about when you want to end a paragraph or insert a blank line?

The answer is that you press the Return or Enter key, and this inserts a character into the stream of letters and spaces to show when the document is printed out that this is where a new paragraph starts. These characters entered by you are called **hard returns** whereas those entered by the program itself to show the ends of lines are called **soft returns**.

TO DO

Still using the document TEST.DOC and starting a new line after your very long sentence, type in the following paragraphs:

One of the most useful features of word processing packages is their ability to wrap round on to the next line automatically when you are typing in.

If a new paragraph is required then simply press the Return key and you will move to a new line.
If a blank line is required, press the Return key once to start a new line and then again to give the blank line.

This is how the spacing looks when using first one Return and then two.

Saving your document

Everything you have typed in so far is only held in the memory of the processor. If the computer were accidentally switched off, or if the power supply failed, all your work would be lost. It is important to find out how to **save** your work as you go along. Usually this command will be easy to remember and use; it may even be permanently displayed on the screen. It is a good idea to get into the habit of saving your work regularly – say after you have typed in each screenful. Then you won't have the frustration of having to start again from scratch if all your work is lost.

What happens when you save?

When you give the command to save, you will first be asked to give your document a filename (unless it has one already). Then the information which you have typed in, which is currently stored in the processor's memory, will be written to the disk which you have specified, under that filename.

TO DO

Find out how to use your word processing package to save a document. Then save what you have done so far on to a disk. Use the name TEST.DOC for the document. Don't use the 'save and exit' command. You want to be able to continue editing.

Scrolling

You will have noticed that as you typed in the paragraphs above, your screen began to fill up with text. Don't worry about this: when the screen is full the text will automatically be **scrolled** up the screen, a line at a time. The text has not disappeared – it is simply stored in the processor's memory. It will return as soon as you try to move the cursor up beyond the top of the screen, and the information you typed earlier will then be scrolled down a line at a time. The same thing will happen if you move the cursor down through a document, or if you move to the right of the screen.

Page wrap

If you were using a typewriter you would easily be able to see when you were running out of space on the piece of paper you are using and need to change this for another. Word processors do this for you. Most tend to default to the A4 size of paper. This will take 66 lines of writing, although allowing for top and bottom margins usually reduces this to about 54. Suppose you set the page length to 54 lines: as you type in the program will automatically wrap line 55 round on to the next page of the document (in much the same way that it wraps round at the end of a line). Usually a line will appear across the screen to mark the end of a page so that you can make sure that it occurs in a logical position in the text. The page number may also be displayed on the status line.

The diagram shows a screen with the line indicating the start of a new page marked across it. Clearly, the page break will follow 'Mrs P Francis – Refreshments'; 'Mr M Riley' will be on a new page.

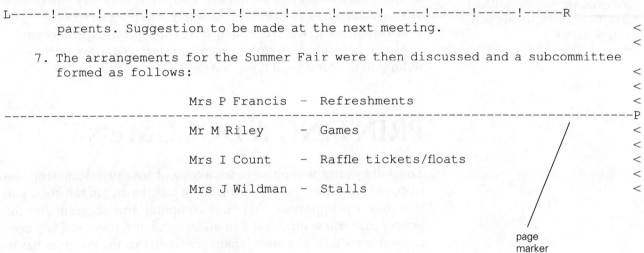

```
    A:MINS.BK    P02 L05 C01 Insert Align
┌──────────────────────── E D I T   M E N U ──────────────────────┐
│   CURSOR           SCROLL           ERASE          OTHER                MENUS           │
│^E up          ^W up           ^G char      ^J help           ^O onscreen format│
│^X down        ^Z down         ^T word      ^I tab            ^K block & save   │
│^S left        ^R up screen    ^Y line      ^V turn insert off ^P print controls│
│^D right       ^C down         Del char     ^B align paragraph ^Q quick functions│
│^A word left      screen       ^U unerase   ^N split the line  Esc shorthand    │
│^F word right                               ^L find/replace again              │
└────────────────────────────────────────────────────────────────┘
L-----!-----!-----!-----!-----!-----!-----!-----! ----!-----!-----!-----R
```

> parents. Suggestion to be made at the next meeting. <
>   <
> 7. The arrangements for the Summer Fair were then discussed and a subcommittee
>   formed as follows: <
>   <
>   Mrs P Francis - Refreshments   <
> --P
>   Mr M Riley   - Games   <
>   <
>   Mrs I Count   - Raffle tickets/floats <
>   <
>   Mrs J Wildman - Stalls   <

page
marker

TO DO

Find out what the page length is set to in your word processing package, and how to change it.

As with paragraphs, there are 'hard' and 'soft' page markers. The program inserts the **soft page breaks,** and you can insert a **hard page break** – perhaps when you do not want a piece of text breaking up, or you need to leave a page for a diagram or something.

You will need to look up the command for inserting a hard page break in your manual, as this is not the same on all word processors.

Setting page lengths and margins

Most of the practice documents in this book are not very long, and you will not need to worry about changing page lengths or margins to begin with. Later on you may decide that you do not like the way that the information in a document is printed out and want to change it. This will mean that you will be changing the default settings for **page length, bottom margin** and **top margin.** Later you may wish to alter some of the features of the printed output (see page 80). To change any of these you will need to look up the right commands in your manual, or ask your teacher.

Make a note of the commands for inserting hard page breaks and for changing the page length and the margins (top and bottom, right and left).

Some word processing packages are known as WYSIWYG. This means 'What You See Is What You Get' – in other words, the print will look exactly like the text you can see on the screen.

Warning! Often you will not be able to see the exact layout of your document as it will be printed, on the screen. This is because you obviously cannot see a whole page at a time, the top and bottom margins are not shown, the line spacing is not shown and the typeface and pitch (the number of characters per inch) are not altered on the screen when you set the values which you want for printing. The only way you can tell exactly what your document will look like is to print it out – but do try to be careful not to waste too many pieces of paper in experimenting!

As you become more experienced you start to know exactly what settings to use for a good layout on the page.

PRINTING A DOCUMENT

You will by now be wanting to see a copy of your first document, and to do this you must print the document out. Earlier in the book you saw that it is important that your computer and program and the printer that you want to use can understand one another. They need to be able to 'talk' the same language. To do this the program has to be **set up** to use your printer. Sometimes this is done when the word processing package is installed, and sometimes you can choose the printer you want while you are actually using it.

TO DO

Make sure that the printer is connected properly to the processor, that it is plugged in to the power supply and that it is **on line**. Get someone to help you do this for the first time, and check that you are using a printer for which the word processing package is set up. You will also probably need help in loading paper into the printer for the first few times.

Don't be afraid to ask how to do this type of thing. But when you do, make a note of exactly what your helper did. And ask questions about anything you don't understand, so that the next time you can try it yourself.

Now you are ready to give the print command from your program and print out TEST.DOC.

When you give the command 'print' you may be asked some questions about how you would like the document printed out – one page at a time, and so on. Make a note of these and choose what you think you want before printing starts.

If you are using continuous stationery, don't forget to turn the printer off line before removing your hard copy from it.

Pitch and character spacing

When printing out your document, try varying the **pitch** setting on the

10   This is Letter Gothic 10 Pitch (14 Point).

12   This is Letter Gothic 12 Pitch (12 Point).

16   This is Letter Gothic 16 Pitch (9.5 Point).

POINT

A A A

36 Point   24 Point   14 Point

Pitch and point

printer. This sets the number of letters which are printed in a given space – usually still quoted in characters per inch: '12 pitch' will give 12 characters per inch and '15 pitch' 15 characters. You may also notice that some word processing packages produce neater print-outs than others do. This may be due to the quality of the printer used, or to the use of **proportional spacing** for the letters. Proportional spacing takes account of the difference in the breadths of letters (for example, 'i' is much narrower than 'w') and spaces out the text accordingly. The height of the characters is measured in **points** – there are 72 points to the inch. The sample of printing at the top of this page shows several different pitches and point sizes, and the one below shows use of proportional and non-proportional spacing.

```
This paragraph illustrates the difference between a fixed space
font and a proportional font. Both versions of the paragraph use a
10 point font, so the individual characters are the same height,
but the first version uses fixed 12 pitch (12 characters per inch)
spacing whilst the second uses proportional spacing. For example,
the space occupied by the letter m is greater in the proportional
font, whereas the space occupied by i is less.
mmmmmmmmmmmmm
iiiiiiiiiiii
```

This paragraph illustrates the difference between a fixed space font and a proportional font. Both versions of the paragraph use a 10 point font, so the individual characters are the same height, but the first version uses fixed 12 pitch (12 characters per inch) spacing whilst the second uses proportional spacing. For example, the space occupied by the letter m is greater in the proportional font, whereas the space occupied by i is less.
mmmmmmmmmmmmm
iiiiiiiiiiii

The effect of proportional spacing

Justification

Compare these two print-outs. Both were produced using a word processing program.

Example 1

```
This document is to show the difference between typing when
RIGHT JUSTIFICATION is set on and when it is set off. There
will be a difference which can be seen along the right-hand
margin of the text which will be straight when right
justification is on and ragged when it is not on.
```

Example 2

```
What is being typed now is the same document which is to show
the difference between having right justification set on and
right justification set off. There will be a difference which
can be seen along the right-hand margin of the text which will
be straight when right justification is set on and ragged when
it is not.
```

You can see that in the first one the right-hand side of the text is 'ragged'. In the second example the right-hand side is **aligned** or **justified** – it looks straight. There are no split words in either example – wordwrap has worked properly in both.

Example 1 was produced with **right justification** set *off*, and Example 2 with right justification *on*.

In both these examples the left side of the text is justified and so Example 2, with two straight edges, is described as **fully justified**.

Justification works by the program keeping a count of the letters and spaces you key in. It then decides what can fit on a line and moves the words along so that the right-hand edge is straight, inserting extra spaces so that the best layout is created. Some people like to use right justification and some think it looks rather artificial. The main problem is that sometimes a particular line or word ends up looking very 'spaced out' as a result. But for, say, a theatre programme or other document where layout and balance are important, you might feel it would be desirable to have a clean right-hand edge.

TO DO

You are now ready to move on to the next exercise. But before you do, you must save the document TEST.DOC and prepare to edit a new document.

You may decide that you should now exit the word processor and practise calling up the program and starting a new document. Or you may decide simply to use a different 'save' command which will allow you to move on to your next piece of work.

Now set up your margins and Tabs and set right justification ON. Use the settings that you think are right for this piece of work.

Type in the memo shown at the top of the next page, without bothering about any mistakes you may make. (In the next section you will be shown how to move around your document and make corrections.)

```
MEMO TO: MR D BLACKHURST
FROM: SUPERVISOR - SEMI-SKIMMED MILK PRODUCTION
SUBJECT: LOSS OF PRODUCTION
DATE: MONDAY 23 JANUARY
```

Owing to a fault in the bottle sterilising equipment the production of semi-skimmed milk has been reduced. We cannot, therefore, supply you with your normal Tuesday allowance of 1000 bottles of semi-skimmed and have substituted 200 bottles of full skimmed instead.

Please apologise to your customers for the substitution.

When you have finished typing the document, save it to a disk under the name MILK.MEM.

Saving and backups

Most word processing packages allow you to keep not one but two copies of a document on disk. The first copy is created the first time you save the document – a space may even be created on the disk for it as soon as you give it a name. The second copy is created the next time you save the document. When this happens the first copy is renamed with the BAK extension and the same filename, and the new copy takes the original filename.

For example, when you create TEST.DOC and save this for the first time, the file TEST.DOC will appear on the directory listing on your disk. If you then type some extra information into the file and save it again you will find.

TEST.DOC
TEST.BAK

both on the directory listing. The BAK file is the older one. Since extra information has been added, it will also be the smaller.

This means that if you lose the most recent copy of your file, you can always go back and work on the **backup** copy, although this may not have all the most recent alterations in it.

TO DO

Have a look at the directory listing of the disk you have been using to save your work on, and see if you can spot two TEST files. If you can't, try saving the file again and then take another look at the listing.

Make sure that the name you use to recall the document is *exactly the same* as the name you used to save it in the first place.

Recalling a document

One of the advantages of word processing is that providing you have saved your document to disk you can always get it back and make changes to it. This is particularly useful where you are likely to use **standard** letters or documents which are needed time and time again.

When you start up your word processing package all you need to do is instead of creating a new file you enter the name of an existing file. The program will look for it and bring it back into the processor's memory.

Load the document MILK.MEM, ready to make any corrections it needs.

Making corrections

Correcting mistakes is far easier with a word processing package on a computer than when you are using a typewriter. Few people are accurate typists, and it is often frustrating to try to use a correcting fluid or paper – and the end result never looks that good.

Insert and overwrite

On the status line displayed on your screen you may be able to see the word 'insert' or 'overwrite'. These indicate the way in which your computer is going to deal with corrections you make. If the **insert** mode is on then anything you type in will be inserted into the existing text at the point where the cursor is positioned. For example, look at the following:

This sentence has seven words in it.

This sentence has seven plus two words in it.

The second sentence has had the words 'plus two' inserted before 'words'. I did this by positioning the cursor on the start of words and then typing in the extra ('plus two') so that it was inserted into the text.

If I had positioned the cursor in the same place but with the **overwrite** mode on, the result would have been:

This sentence has seven plus two it.

The eight characters in the words 'plus two' have overwritten the existing characters in 'words in', and the sentence no longer makes sense.

Always set 'overwrite' or 'insert' *before* making corrections, or even entering text to begin with. Usually the default setting is 'insert' (sometimes described as **push** mode).

TO DO

Make the following changes to the file MILK.MEM:

1 Insert the word 'milk' before 'instead' on the last line of the first paragraph.
2 Insert a blank line after each of the four lines in the heading.
3 Insert the following into the first sentence after the word 'equipment':
  'which occurred on Saturday night,'.
4 Insert the following sentence after the word 'reduced' (line 2):
  'The supply may well not reach its normal level for another two days while we await the delivery of a new part for the machine.'
5 Save your memo.
6 Print your memo.
7 Your memo should now look like the print-out shown here.

```
MEMO TO: MR D BLACKHURST
FROM : SUPERVISOR - SEMI-SKIMMED MILK PRODUCTION
SUBJECT: LOSS OF PRODUCTION
DATE: MONDAY 23 JANUARY

Owing to a fault in the bottle sterilising equipment which occurred
on Saturday night, the production of semi-skimmed milk has been
reduced. The supply may well not reach its normal level for another
two days while we await the delivery of a new part for the machine.
We cannot, therefore, supply you with your normal Tuesday allowance
of 1000 bottles of semi-skimmed and have substituted 200 bottles of
full skimmed milk instead.

Please apologise to your customers for the substitution.
```

Splitting paragraphs

One correction that you may need to do is to split a paragraph into
two. This is done by inserting a 'hard return' character, plus a Tab
mark if you like to use one, at the place where you want the paragraph splitting.

'Hard returns' are Return characters which are entered by the user. Those entered by the program itself to show ends of lines are called 'soft returns'.

TO DO

Split the first paragraph in MILK.MEM into two, inserting a blank
line in between the two new paragraphs, after the sentence which
ends 'part for the machine.' Save the corrected memo.

Moving the cursor

The cursor shows you your position on the screen. There are lots of
ways in which you can move the cursor around a document.

TO DO

Find out how to use the following features of a word processing
package, what the commands are on your package and what they do:

- page up
- page down
- end
- home

- top of document
- end of document
- word right
- word left.

Most of the commands you need will use the **function keys**, either
alone or in combination with the Shift, Ctrl or Alt keys.

If a command involves using a combination of keys, say the Shift and F5 keys, make sure that you press down the Shift key first and *hold it down* while you press the F5 key. Don't try to press both at once: you will find that your co-ordination isn't good enough and you may end up giving a totally different command from the one you intended.

Deleting text

From time to time you will probably need to delete or get rid of characters, words or sections of your document. There are several commands which will be available to you for this. There will be two keys
on the keyboard you can use – the **backspace** (Bksp), which deletes
the character immediately behind the cursor position, and the **delete**
(Del) key, which deletes the character *at* the cursor position.

There will also be commands for deleting whole words and lines of
text, and even whole paragraphs.

Merging paragraphs together

Quite often you will find that you want to get rid of the space between two paragraphs and turn them into just one. All you have to do is to get rid of the special character which the program will have inserted when you pressed the Return key (hard return). Simply position your cursor on the first letter of the second paragraph, and press the backspace key once. This will delete the Return before the beginning of the paragraph. If you separated the two paragraphs with a blank line then you will need to press the backspace key twice, to get rid of the second 'hard return' character.

TO DO (1)

Find out the Delete commands that you can use with your word processor. (Look in your manual or ask your teacher.)

TO DO (2)

Brown Owl has prepared this letter for the Brownies to take home but has realised that she has missed some things out. Type in the letter as it is and then make the alterations described underneath. Save the document when you have typed it (give it the filename BROWN.LET) before you make the corrections.

BROWNIES TRIP TO SOUTHPORT

The Brownie Pack holiday this year will be to Southport on the 1st to the 3rd of June.

The coach will depart at 5.30 p.m. on the 1st and return at approximately 5.00 p.m. on the 3rd.

A meeting will be held for parents on Monday 22nd April in the school hall to give further information.

If you would like your daughter to join us on the trip please send a deposit of five pounds by Monday 15th March.

Corrections
1 State that the coach will leave from and return to the Crown car park.
2 Add in that places are limited and so will be given to those who bring in their deposits first.
3 Include a note that the deposit is non-refundable.
4 Change the date by which deposits must be paid to Monday 18th March.

TO DO (3)

Prepare a similar letter for an organisation or club of which you are a member, or for an office outing.

Marking text

One useful feature of a word processor is the ability to mark **blocks** of text, which you can then move, copy or delete with just a few keystrokes. These blocks can be part of a paragraph, or one or more whole paragraphs.

Your word processor will have commands which allow you to **mark** the start and end of the block you want to work with, and then separate commands for copying, deleting and moving.

Some word processing manuals describe the process of marking and moving text as **cutting and pasting** – as if you were actually cutting out pieces of writing and pasting them back together in a new order.

TO DO

Create a file called BLOCK.EXS and type in the following rather mixed-up extract from a book called *Mastering Word Processing* by Peter and Joanna Gosling.

PRACTICE MAKES PERFECT!

It is often felt, by people unfamiliar with this very useful application of the new technology, that there is so much to remember and so many new things to learn, apart from the geography of the keyboard, that it offers no real advantage over the typewriter.

All word processors will allow you top perform a series of basic word manipulations, but some will offer a number of sophisticated additional functions, some of which you may need desparately and some of which you may find of no use at all.

You will make the most dreadful mistakes in the early stages and trhe whole thing will appear to be a blur until suddenly the end of the tunnel appears and you will wonder what all the fuss was about.

The keystrokes needed to perform the common word processing functions on your chosen system The keystrokes needed to perform the common word processing functions on your chosen system are usually very easy to memorise as they generally falll into a recognisable pattern.

Remember always to read what is on the screen and . . .

Make the following alterations to the passage above:

1 Move the second paragraph before the first.
2 Correct the spelling mistakes.
3 Get rid of the repeated section at the start of the fourth paragraph.
4 Copy the title line to a suitable position below the last line of the text.
5 Swop paragraphs three and four over.

Spelling

Most people make mistakes when typing in, and often spelling mistakes can be hard to spot when checking and correcting documents. For this reason, many word processing packages include a spell checker which allows users to check their documents for spelling mistakes.

Remember that a spell checker will not pick up the misuse of words. For example, 'practice' and 'practise' are both correct spellings – but mean different things!

You should now be able to:

☐ recall and correct a document

☐ use your word processing package to move around a document, insert, delete and copy.

It is partly because of these special characters that your printer has to be properly set up for use with your word processing package. It has to be made to understand the code.

The Print characters may be shown on the screen as you type, in which case What You See Is *not* What You Get (see page 72). If the text is highlighted or coloured and the characters are not shown, then WYSIWYG!

TO DO

Find out if your word processing package includes a spell checker. If so, try using it.

Search and replace

Sometimes you will find you have made the same spelling mistake throughout a document, or realise you have given the wrong name to a place or person. If you want to correct a series of mistakes like this, or if your document is a long one and you want to find a point in it quickly, the **search** and **replace** commands are useful.

TO DO

Look up how to use the 'search and replace' commands. Find the word 'mistakes' in the exercise BLOCK.EXS, and replace it with 'errors'.

Making it all look good

So far you will have concentrated on getting information entered, edited, saved and printed but will not have thought very much about what the completed document is going to look like.

Some of the features already covered, such as justification, the setting of margins, the use of Tabs for indentation and the use of blank lines at appropriate places, will help with the **look** of the completed document. There are, however, other features which can be used to improve presentation. These are sometimes known as Print or Dot commands. A special character is entered into the stream of text to indicate, for example, when text is to be underlined or when bold type is to be used. The special characters usually work as switches: for example, the first time a 'bold' character is inserted, bold type is switched on. When the next 'bold' character is read, bold type is switched off.

TO DO

Find out what commands are available in your own word processing package. Look particularly for **bold**, **underline** and **centre**.

TO DO(1)

Look at the example of what is known as a **fly sheet** or mini poster.
Create a file called HORSE.FLY and enter the text as shown.
You will need to use the commands for **centre**, **bold** and **underline**.
Save and print out your fly sheet.

THE GRANGE RIDING CLUB
ANNUAL SHOW

SATURDAY 6 SEPTEMBER

AT

THE STABLES
STATION ROAD
EQUIVALE

by kind permission of Mr and Mrs R Wood

Classes start 9.30 a.m. PROMPT

REFRESHMENTS AVAILABLE

To include: Ridden and in hand classes, Gymkhana Games,
Show Jumping

SCHEDULES FROM:
Mrs L Hock
Coronet House
Cannon Street
Pastern

TO DO (2)

Now design a similar poster for an event which you will be involved in.

Inserting a file

In the following exercise on preparing a set of minutes you will create two separate files and then copy one into the other.

This is the sort of thing which you can't possibly do using a typewriter, short of physically cutting and pasting documents together or retyping the whole thing.

How you do this will depend on the commands in your own word processing package. You will probably find the instructions under **inserting** or **copying** of text. Make sure that you have *both* files typed in and saved before you try inserting the second one into the first.

The ability to perform this moving around and insertion of whole files lets you build up a document from a set of standard paragraphs, each kept in a different file, so that the completed document will be suitable for your particular needs.

For example, think of the letters sent out from a company when it receives orders – sometimes the goods are in stock and can be sent straight away, sometimes there is a delay to tell the customer about, sometimes the customer has ordered discontinued stock. In all these letters, some of the paragraphs will probably be the same. For instance:

Thank you for your order which we received today.

We hope that you will continue to do business with Bloggs and Sons.

and even

May we take this opportunity to inform you of some of our new products, which will be available from 20 November this year.

or

Mr Frederick Bloggs and his sons Albert and Richard would like to wish everyone at Robinson and Daughters a happy Christmas and prosperous New Year.

TO DO

Complete the exercise on minutes as described below. You will need to set your page length, margins and Tab positions very carefully before you start. Remember that these must be the same for *both* documents. See if you can improve the appearance of the minutes by using bold type or by centering some of the headings.

As Mr Scribe, secretary of your local Parent Teachers Association, you have the job of preparing the minutes of the last meeting. Key in the following text on your word processor for printing out and distribution to the rest of the committee. Save it under the filename PTA.MIN.

MINUTES OF A MEETING OF THE OVER PEVERO PARENT TEACHERS ASSOCIATION

19 FEBRUARY 1991

Present: Chairperson   – Mrs J Robinson
        Vice Chair   – Mr J Holland
        Secretary   – Mr A Scribe
        Treasurer   – Mrs I Count
        Parent Members   – Mr L Hooper
                        – Mrs P Francis
                        – Mr D Wilson
                        – Mr P Lawrence
                        – Mrs E Billington
                        – Mrs P Roberts
        Teaching Staff   – Miss P Jeffs (Head)
                        – Mr M Riley
                        – Mrs S Ray

1 Apologies were received from: Mr I Gregory
                                   Mrs J Wildman

2 The minutes of the last meeting were accepted as read – proposed by Mr L Hooper, seconded by Mrs E Billington.

3 The chairperson reported that work on the provision of a parking area outside school was well under way and that it was hoped that the work would be finished by the end of the Easter holidays.

4 The Treasurer reported that there is currently £538 in the association's funds, £500 in the deposit account and £38 in the current account.

The proceeds from the Christmas raffle were £146.

5 The arrangements for the Family Fun Day are well under way. Mr Holland has booked the Leisure Centre for 20 April and he and Mrs Roberts are organising the games and equipment.

6 The teaching staff were asked to decide what they would most like the PTA to purchase for the school from any funds raised by the Summer Fair so that this can be explained to the parents. Suggestion to be made at the next meeting.

7 The arrangements for the Summer Fair were then discussed and a subcommittee formed as follows:

Mrs P Francis – Refreshments
Mr M Riley – Games
Mrs I Count – Raffle tickets/floats
Mrs J Wildman – Stalls

8 Date of the next meeting – 14 April in the school hall at 8 p.m.

Meeting closed at 9.45 p.m.

When Mr Scribe prepared the minutes of the PTA meeting he wrote a separate note which could be used for Mrs Wildman and which he could then add in to the minutes to save him typing it in twice.

Type in this extra note under the filename EXTRA.MIN, save it, then recall the minutes PTA.MIN and insert this extra information into point 7 together with the other details about the Summer Fair. Save the new minutes under the name NEW.MIN.

NOTE FOR MRS WILDMAN
Suggested list of stalls for Summer Fair – to be passed to Mrs Wildman by Mrs Billington.

Tombola
Cakes
Bric-a-Brac
Children's Tombola
Plants and Garden Produce
Toys and Games
Books

Stalls could also be run by other local organisations who would be expected to donate 10% of their proceeds to the School. These stalls NOT to clash with any of ours.

APPLICATIONS OF WORD PROCESSING PACKAGES

By now you should be able to see where a word processing package can help in your work at school or college or at home. You will find it easy to produce any type of standard letter or form, and the job will only need doing once. You will be able to produce your own curriculum vitae or profile, and your letters will look professional.

The more you use your word processing package the easier it will become, and then you will want to find out about some of the more complicated things which these packages can be used for – like mail shots and address labels.

Once you feel confident with using a word processing package, you are ready to move on to the next chapter. This deals with **databases**.

8 · STORING AND FILING INFORMATION: DATABASES

In the last section of the book you saw how to create information using a word processor. But what about all the information you already have which needs storing, sorting and filing? Is there any way in which computers can help with this?

The answer is yes, there is! The application software which is used for this type of work is known simply as a **database package**. Its full title is **database management package**, as the software itself does not contain data but provide the means to store, sort and file it.

In this chapter you will learn why we need to be able to store, sort and file information and how this is done using a database package. By the time you have worked through the chapter you should be able to design and build your own computerised database and extract information from it.

WHY DO WE NEED INFORMATION?

The society we live in today has become known as the **information society**. All of us have – and want – access to information for pleasure, home and work. At school or college much of your work will be based on finding out about things, and you will have access to far more information about the world than ever before.

Businesses now operate across countries and continents, or even worldwide. They need up-to-the-minute information on costs of raw materials, labour and so forth so that they can use their resources as efficiently as possible. They also need information about people and what they want to buy, how much they want to pay and so on. This type of information is used in making decisions that affect the growth and profit of a company.

Collecting and analysing information has itself become big business, with companies specialising in just that. But having lots of information is no use at all unless that information is **organised** in a way that is easy and quick to use.

STORING INFORMATION

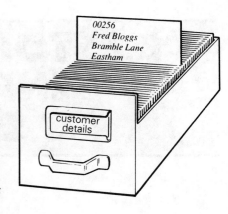

As people, organisations and businesses acquire more and more information, they all have to find ways of storing it.

Take, for example, someone setting up in business selling made-to-measure clothes. To begin with they might simply keep a list of their clients in a notebook or address book with the odd detail about them scribbled down. Probably little else is needed, as with only a few customers the dressmaker is likely to remember them all. As the business expands, a **card index system** could be introduced, where details of each client are kept on a separate card. The cards are filed in a box in some sort of order, and extracted when needed.

But the card index used to record clients' details is only coping with one type of information. Other types of information will need to be stored too – for example, invoices and receipts, details of materials suppliers, patterns made for customers' clothes and all sorts of other things. Perhaps the solution to this might be a filing cabinet with lots of drawers, one for each type of information.

TO DO

Imagine you are starting up a business of your own. Write down all the different types of information you would need.

There are many different ways of storing information available today, ranging from the simple card index or address book to the microfilm or fiche used in libraries. What method is chosen will depend on:

- the amount of information to be stored
- the type of information
- the speed and ease of access to the information that is required
- the security needed for the information
- how often the information needs updating or changing

and

- the amount of money available to pay for it!

TO DO

Think of as many ways as you can of how people store information. Can you see why each method is used? Look for the different methods at home, at work, at school, out shopping, at the doctor's or dentist's, and so on.

You should now be able to:

☐ understand why large amounts of information are used in modern society

☐ give examples of storage techniques and understand why they are used.

CLASSIFYING INFORMATION

How am I supposed to know Mr Marsden is filed under GOLF CLUB ?

There is not much point in storing information unless you can find what you want when you want it!

To get round this problem, various methods of **classifying** information have been introduced. For information which is going to be used by more than one person it is usually best to use one of the recognised methods. Otherwise you may find that only you can use the system!

Address books and telephone directories are organised in **alphabetical** order to make it easy and quick to find the details you require (the only problem here being if you do not know a person's surname).

Example

In a telephone directory people's names are organised **alphabetically by surname**. All the surnames starting with B come after all those starting with A. Also

BROWN, ERNEST

will come before

BROWN, WILLIAM

as they are organised alphabetically by first name as well.

There are lots of ways in which information can be classified to make it easier to find. Here are some of the most common:

- a guide book on hotels or towns may be organised **geographically** by county or region

- orders for goods received at a factory might be classified **chronologically** (time) based on the date the order was received

- items of stock in a shop may be classified **numerically,** based on a stock number

- in a bookshop books could be classified by **subject** (for example, sport, travel, cooking, fiction and so on).

TO DO

Think of the ways in which you classify information at home. Do you have a hobby where you need to keep records of what you collect? How do you keep bills, insurance details, bank statements and so forth?

You will probably have found that you automatically **classify and file** many pieces of information. If you don't, you are likely to waste a lot of time looking for lost information!

INDEXES

Once you have a collection of information which is classified in some way, it is often useful to use an **index** to make finding a piece of information quicker. This is not always true; it depends on the type of classification you have used.

For example, an index is not needed in the main part of a telephone directory because all the individual pieces of information are set out in order. But in a recipe book where the recipes are classified by subject (soups, puddings, meat and so on) it could take a long time to find an individual recipe for say, chicken soup. So an index to the recipes themselves is often included. Of course, actually preparing an index like this manually is a time-consuming business, and if the information changes frequently it can be difficult to keep the index up to date.

Example
The made-to-measure clothes business could use a filing system based on a filing cabinet in which files or cards holding the customers' names and other details are kept in alphabetical order, with an index to the drawers of the cabinet giving the range of surnames in each drawer.

TO DO

Think about how you keep your address book up to date as friends move, or you lose touch with some and make new ones.

Visit your local library, and have a look at the classification and indexing systems used there.

You should now be able to:

☐ classify information with which you are familiar

☐ understand why information is classified and indexed.

DATABASES

We saw that the small made-to-measure clothing business needed several types of information, each of which might be classified and indexed separately. This kind of collection of various types of information or data which are related in some way is usually called a **database**. In this example the data is that necessary for the working of that small business, and might include a customer file, a suppliers file, an accounts file, a stock file and a designs file.

Large systems

Most of the examples used so far are of fairly small filing systems dealing with relatively small amounts of information. But even with these you will be beginning to see some of the problems arising in their maintenance and use. Imagine the problems where very large amounts of information are involved!

Imagine, for example, a large insurance company, which files and classifies information on each of its policy holders. A clerk takes a phone call about a customer's policy and has to go and search for the

In simple terms a database is a collection of one or more files, which are usually related.

correct file and bring it back before he can answer the query – which will usually mean having to take a message, get the file and then ring back. While that clerk has the file, of course, no one else can get hold of it. If a different clerk is then asked to update the information on that customer, she won't be able to deal with it until the file is returned – and how will she know when that will be without making lots of trips to the place where the files are stored? She probably won't be allowed actually to wander into the area where files are stored, so on each visit she will have to queue to get her enquiry answered.

And the situation will be even worse if the company has offices scattered all round the country but maintains the files on policy holders centrally. Branch managers who need information on a customer would have to either send for the file or get copies made – and then updating and maintenance becomes even more difficult.

TO DO

From which large centralised information systems have you used information? Make a list.

Getting access to large amounts of data quickly and efficiently is an essential part of many companies' business and necessary to their survival – whether it is manufacturing companies trying to minimise production costs, distribution companies trying to keep information on large fleets of vehicles, or supermarket chains trying to keep stocks to a minimum without losing trade.

How do organisations like these manage to keep all the information they store up to date and easily accessible? The answer is described in the next section.

COMPUTERISED DATABASE MANAGEMENT SYSTEMS

Computers clearly can offer us an enormous amount of help in storing information while allowing easy access, sorting and retrieval of that information. Without computerised database systems it would not be possible for banks to operate their 'holes in the wall' or for travel operators to arrange our holidays speedily. Flights could be overbooked on planes, people could become badly overdrawn on their bank accounts and companies could fail to compete in this increasingly information-hungry world.

Sometimes it is difficult to tell which came first – the need or the computerised systems. Certainly, however, the more information people have the more they want, and the quicker a system works the faster it is required to!

The advantages of electronic database systems are tremendous. You realise this more clearly when you have used one for yourself.

Being able to access large amounts of data quickly and efficiently is something which we all need today.

USING A COMPUTERISED DATABASE PACKAGE

Understanding the terminology

When you are using a database package for the first time, you may have some problems with the terms used in the manual. But it is important that you understand exactly what each term means, or you will find yourself getting in a muddle. So spend some time in reading and thinking about this section before you go any further.

Files, records and fields

Our made-to-measure clothes business will need to keep information on each of its customers. What information should be kept? What would be useful to the efficient running of the business?

The following are some of the pieces of information which would be kept for each customer:

- full name
- address
- postcode
- telephone number(s).

Additionally information on the following might be included:

- measurements
- colour preference
- comments on style of clothes preferred
- would/would not agree to be used in sales literature/photos.

TO DO

Design a record card to keep the above information in a card index file.

A file is made up of records.

All the information on all the customers would make up the customer file, and the information on one customer would be one **record** on the file.

Each record is in turn made up of several items of information. In the example above the items listed are full name, address and so on. When you designed the record card for this information, how did you do it? Did you have all the address written on one line? Did you separate off the customer's first name or initials from the surname? Suppose you are looking for all the customers who live in a particular town, so that they could be invited to come to a fashion show; how easy would it be to search through the cards for their names, if the town is muddled up somewhere in the address line? It would probably be better to lay the information out something like this:

```
SURNAME:
FIRST NAME(s):

HOUSE NAME OR NUMBER:
ROAD:
TOWN:
COUNTY:
POSTCODE:
TELEPHONE HOME:
TELEPHONE WORK:

MEASUREMENTS:

COLOURS PREFERRED:
STYLES PREFERRED:

USE IN PUBLICITY MATERIAL? Y/N
```

In database language, each of these items is called a **field**. All of the fields together make up one customer **record**. A record is made up of one or more fields. An example of an actual record is shown below:

```
SURNAME:                  SMART
FIRST NAME(s):            IRIS

HOUSE NAME OR NUMBER:     ROAMINDUN
ROAD:                     HIGH ROAD
TOWN:                     FRENSHAM
COUNTY:                   BERKS
POSTCODE:                 RD2 5PQ
TELEPHONE HOME:           0456-12345
TELEPHONE WORK:           0467-23456

MEASUREMENTS:             WAIST: 26, BUST: 36, HIPS: 36

COLOURS PREFERRED:        BLUE, PINK, GREEN
STYLES PREFERRED:         CASUAL

USE IN PUBLICITY MATERIAL? Y
```

The **field names** are the headings surname, postcode and so on, and the details for the customer, such as SMART and RD2 5PQ, are the **contents of the fields**.

Some records are made up of many short fields. For example, here is a record from a file of stock kept by a chain of fashion stores:

```
STOCK NUMBER         BW1234231
QUANTITY HELD        20
REORDER LEVEL        5
REORDER QUANTITY     25
TIME DELAY           2
PRICE TO US          20
FOR SALE PRICE       35
STORE                M
SHELF                37
DISCOUNT             N
SUPPLIER             345
COLOUR               DB
WAIST SIZE           24
LENGTH               28
DESCRIPTION          WOMENS FINE CORD JEANS FRONT
                     POCKETS ONE POCKET ON BACK RIGHT
                     TAILORED FIT
```

In this record, many of the fields and their contents seem at first sight to mean very little. This is because the person who designed the **record structure** obviously decided to use codes, so that the information would take up less space and be easier to use, as the amount of typing or writing is much reduced. For example, the field named STORE shows which warehouse the goods are stored in, and the M stands for Manchester. If the goods were stored in Leeds then the code would be L, and so on. In the same way the contents of all the fields representing prices are shown only as whole numbers, with no pound signs or pence included. Anyone knowing the system understands that prices are quoted in pounds, without bothering over pence – it is a policy of the company.

The next example shows quite a different type of record. Here the fields contain long items of text rather than simple figures and codes.

```
SURNAME       BONES
FIRST NAME    LESLIE ARTHUR
CLASS         2B
YEAR          1992-93

ART           WORK IS SLOPPY, NEVER FINISHED, MAKES A
              MESS IN THE WORK ROOM, OFTEN TOLD OFF FOR
              TALKING AND DISTRACTING OTHERS

BIOLOGY       NO PROGRESS MADE THIS YEAR, LESLIE NEEDS TO
              BUCKLE DOWN TO SOME HARD WORK IF THERE IS
              TO BE ANY POINT AT ALL IN HIM ATTENDING MY
              LESSONS

CHEMISTRY     LESLIE HAS NOT BOTHERED TO DO ANY OF THE
              HOMEWORK SET. HE SPENDS MOST OF HIS TIME
              ACCIDENTALLY TRYING TO BLOW UP THE LAB
              SIMPLY BY FAILING TO FOLLOW INSTRUCTIONS –
              HE IS A HAZARD TO OTHER PUPILS

FRENCH        IF LESLIE SPENT LESS TIME STARING OUT OF
              THE WINDOW AND MORE ON CONCENTRATING ON THE
              TASK IN HAND HE MIGHT MAKE PROGRESS

MATHS         LESLIE FINDS THE SUBJECT EASY AND SO LONG
              AS HE IS NOT EXPECTED TO DO ANY HOMEWORK IS
              QUITE HAPPY. HE IS PERFECTLY CAPABLE OF
              COMPLETING THE WORK WHICH IS SET BUT JUST
              DOESN'T BOTHER TO MAKE THE EFFORT
```

TO DO

Design a record structure for some information which you want to keep. This means working out what fields you would want to use. Bear in mind that you may want to sort the records in some way, and decide which fields you might want to sort them on.

A database is a collection of data or information often related in some way (for example, all the information needed by a company). It usually consists of a series of files.

A file contains a set of records.

A record is made up of one or more fields.

Fixed-length and variable-length records

When you designed the record card for the customer information for the made-to-measure clothes business you probably tried to organise the fields in such a way that you left a reasonable amount of space for the different items. For example, you would know that a telephone number is unlikely to take up more than 12 to 14 spaces whereas the details of preferred colours could be a single word or a whole description. Similarly, if you were designing a manual filing system you would need to make allowances for the differing lengths of fields. The same is true with a computerised system.

In many files of information the records are all the same length, the length of each field and the number of fields that make up a record having been set at the start. This type of record is known as a **fixed-length record**. The stock file record is a good example of a fixed-length record – all the fields in it can be set to a maximum length and all the fields must be filled for each item of stock (that is, for each record on the file).

It is not always possible to say how long the records in a file are going to be, however, and some may be longer than others. For example, think of a file containing records on patients and their visits to a hospital. Some patients will have more visits than others, and it will not be possible to say exactly what length a particular record will be. This type of record is known as a **variable-length record**. Here are two examples.

```
PATIENTS SURNAME     BLOGGS                    PATIENTS SURNAME     WALLIS
FIRST NAMES          FRED                      FIRST NAMES          ARTHUR JOSEPH
DATE FIRST ADMITTED  12/03/68                  DATE FIRST ADMITTED  08/01/76
FIRST VISIT          12/03/68 SLIPPED ON       FIRST VISIT          08/01/76 WHIPLASH
                     ICE, STRAINED MUSCLE                           INJURY CAUSED BY
                     IN BACK. X-RAYS                                ACCIDENT TO CAR HE
                     TAKEN, NOTHING                                 WAS DRIVING. COLLAR
                     BROKEN, REST ADVISED                           FITTED AND
                                                                    PAINKILLERS
SECOND VISIT         22/09/74 FELL OFF                              DISPENSED. REPORT
                     LADDER IN GARDEN AND                           PROVIDED FOR POLICE
                     CUT HAND BADLY ON                              AND INSURANCE
                     SAW. NO BONES                                  COMPANY
                     BROKEN. TETANUS
                     INJECTION GIVEN AND
                     WOUND CLEANED,
                     STITCHED(6) AND
                     DRESSED

THIRD VISIT          29/09/74 WOUND TO
                     HAND REDRESSED

FOURTH VISIT         05/10/74 STITCHES IN
                     HAND REMOVED AND
                     WOUND REDRESSED
```

You should now be able to:

☐ understand the structure of a database, and see ways in which data with which you are familiar could be structured

☐ remember and understand the following terms: record, field, file, database, fixed- and variable-length records.

Types of information

Before moving on to design and build a database file, we need to consider the **type of information** that is to be kept in each field. The easiest way to understand this is to look at a sample database record and see what type of information is stored in each field.

Example

Field name	Field size	Contents of example record
SURNAME	30	JONES
FIRST NAME	30	NICOLA
AGE	2	24
DATE OF BIRTH	8	18/07/66
POSITION	30	SECRETARY - MARKETING
SKILLS	50	AUDIO TYPING, WPM(65), GERMAN, FRENCH
CAR OWNER	1	Y
SALARY	5	10500

TOTAL LENGTH OF RECORD 156 CHARACTERS

In this example,

- the first two fields and the position field contain **alphabetic** data
- the age and salary fields contain **numeric** data
- the date of birth field contains a **date**
- the skills field contains **alphanumeric** data
- the car owner field can only contain one of two answers, Y or N, and this is sometimes known as **logical** data.

These are the most common types of data found, and most database packages will allow you to use these types. For numeric fields, you may also need to specify that there are decimal places in the figures – for example, in a field containing the price of something in pounds and pence.

TO DO

Use the example data below to prepare a sample record with likely field names, sizes and data types for a file containing records of used cars for sale.

Ford Escort,
1987,
2 door,
1600cc,
red,
extras – sun roof, stereo, sports wheels, 4 speakers
price £3500,
taxed? yes (standard 1 year),
MOT? yes, to 01/10/92.

Record size

In the example of the employee details at the top of this page, a length was given for each of the fields. This is a *maximum* expected length for the field, and is given so that enough space may be reserved for this amount of information. If you were designing a record card for this record, you would have to make sure there was enough space on each line of your record card. In the same way, when you are using a computer you need to tell the program the maximum length of any field.

If you know that the total length of your record is 156 characters and you are likely to have no more than 100 records on the file then you can work out the maximum number of characters (15 600) to be stored, and the amount of space this is likely to take up.

TO DO

For the used car file for which you have designed a record structure, what would be the total maximum length of a record?

If there were never more than 120 cars for sale at any one time, what would be the maximum size of the file?

All the information you have read in this chapter so far can be applied to any database system, whether it is a manual or a computerised one. The next section deals with how to set up and use a computerised system. Before you move on, just stop and think how much planning must go into the design of any file structure before it is set up. The data that is required, how much of it there is, the different fields required, what sort of information they contain and how long they need to be – all of these must be carefully worked out. Otherwise it won't matter whether a computerised system or a manual one is used – if the design is wrong, it just won't work.

You should now be able to:

☐ choose a suitable method for filing information with which you are familiar

☐ design a record structure for the information, giving the type of information to be put into each field

☐ calculate the length of a record and the total length of a file.

SETTING UP A COMPUTERISED DATABASE

The aim of this part of the book is to help you to understand how a computerised database package works, and what one can do for you. You will need to refer to your own manual and/or your teacher to find out the exact commands to use. The database package which is used in the examples is dbase III+, and the instructions are based on using a twin floppy disk computer. You will need to use the information on houses being sold by an estate agent given in the Appendix at the end of this book.

TO DO

Start by looking at the information in the Appendix and working out how you would record these details in a manual record system. Consider:

- the **fields** which will be required
- the **type** of data in each field
- the **size** of each field
- suitable **names** for the fields
- any **codes** which you will use – say   D for detached
                                            S for semi-detached
                                            B for bungalow
                                            T for a terrace house
                                            and so on.

Loading a database package

Look in your manual, or ask your teacher, if you are not sure how to load a database management system piece of software.

The contents of a database package

Some database packages are quite simple, but much of the software on the market today can seem very complicated to the first-time user. Most database packages consist of several types of program, which help you

- to create a database **format**
- to enter data into a file
- to maintain the files
- to search and sort data in the files
- to create special layouts for printing
- to write your own programs (routines) for doing common tasks like producing reports

and so on. You will soon find out all the different functions of your particular database package.

TO DO

Load your database system on your computer. Then find out from your manual or ask your teacher how to create a new database file using your software.

Create a new file called HOUSES.

Database packaged software is often quite complicated and you may find that it comes on not one but two floppy disks. If so, the instructions on the screen will tell you when to insert the second disk into the disk drive.

Some people like to call database packages **database management systems**, as this is what they actually are – they help you to manage the data, they do not actually contain any data themselves. This is why you need the separate data disk, which is where you will store the files you create using the database package.

Creating a database file and a file layout

Now that you know how to **create a file** – in other words tell the program that you are going to make a file with a certain name and that you will want to store information in it in a certain place (for example, on the disk in drive B or drive A) – you need to describe to the program the type of information that is to go into each field and the length of each field. This is the **record layout**, which you should have already prepared.

You will find that the database software allows you only a certain number of different types of data. In dbaseIII+ these are:

- **character** – all the characters on the keyboard are allowed
- **numeric** – only numbers are allowed, with no decimal points; the number of decimal places is filled in as a separate requirement
- **date** – if 'date' is chosen the size of the field is filled in for you automatically as 8; the date has to be in the format mm/dd/yy (month, day, year, separated by / symbols – this, unlike the examples used so far, is the **American date format** used by dbase)

- **logical –**   this is what dbase calls the type of data where there is a choice of only two possible answers – like Y or N
- **memo –**   this type of data field has not yet been mentioned; it is used for the sort of field where you are not sure how much information may be included.

Don't be afraid to ask for help with setting up a record structure. It's important to get the setting up of a database file done correctly – otherwise you could run into problems later.

TO DO

In the particular file we are creating, some records will include a description stating the size and different features of the gardens, while others will not mention gardens at all. See if there is a type of field that will allow you to enter information on the gardens. If not, then simply leave this out from your database.

The screen picture below shows what would be a sensible record layout or format for the data in the Appendix. Notice that:

- there are no spaces in the field names, and there is a maximum length for these
- the fields are numbered
- the width of each field and the type of data in it are given, as is the number of decimal places for each numeric field.

```
                                                    Bytes remaining: 3909

 ┌─────────────────┐ ┌─────────────────┐ ┌─────────────────┐ ┌─────────────────┐
 │ CURSOR ← →      │ │ INSERT          │ │ DELETE          │ │ Up a field      │
 │ : Char ← →      │ │ Char: Ins       │ │ : Char: Del     │ │ Down a field    │
 │ : Word:Home End │ │ : Field: ^N     │ │ : Word: ^Y      │ │ Exit/Save: ^End │
 │ : Pan           │ │ : Help: F1      │ │ : Field: ^U     │ │ Abort: Esc      │
 └─────────────────┘ └─────────────────┘ └─────────────────┘ └─────────────────┘
```

Field Name	Type	Width	Dec		Field Name	Type	Width	Dec
1 TOWN	Character	20			9 GARAGE	Character	1	
2 STREET	Character	20			10 GARDENS	Memo	10	
3 TYPE	Character	1			11 PRICE	Numeric	6	0
4 NOBEDS	Numeric	1	0		12 DATEONBOOK	Date	8	
5 NORECEP	Numeric	1	0		13 OWNERNAME	Character	20	
6 KITCHEN	Logical	1						
7 UTILITY	Logical	1						
8 BATHROOMS	Numeric	1	0					

```
MODIFY STRUCTURE ‹A; ›; HOUSES Field: 1/13
                          Enter the field name.
Field names begin with a letter and may contain letters, digits and underscores
```

Saving the record structure

When you have finished entering all the fields and you have checked them over to make sure they are just what is required then you must **save** the structure, just as you did with your word processing work. You will need to find the correct command to use for this on your database package.

What happens when you set up a record structure?

When you set up the structure or layout of a record in a database, you are providing the database management system with a model for the storing and retrieval of records in the file. When the record structure is stored away it will be stored either as an extra added on to the actual file or as a separate file created by the software.

Remember that computers deal with any information as a stream of characters. So when we enter our first record on to our database file HOUSES it could look something like this:

```
WESTWICH        WILLIAM ST
T22YN10REAR YARD 0400000080190
```

This string of characters (including spaces) could mean anything and it is the record structure, our template, which gives it meaning.

If you didn't have the record structure saved and the imaginary template slipped one character to the right, then a £40 000 house would appear as a £400 000 one!

TO DO

Using the record structure shown above, work out the descriptions of the following properties (remember that the dates are given American-style, mm/dd/yy).

```
CHAPEL HOLME    SPINNEY AVE
D42YN11BEAUTIFUL, WELL STOCKED 1/5TH ACRE
189950041089

WESTWICH  GREENLEY AVENUE
S32YN10LARGE GARDENS WITH PARKING SPACE FOR 2
CARS. SUNLOUNGE OPENS UP ONTO
PATIO087500022890
```

You should now be able to:

☐ design a database
☐ load a database software package
☐ use the package to:
  ● create a database file
  ● create a record layout
  ● save a record layout.

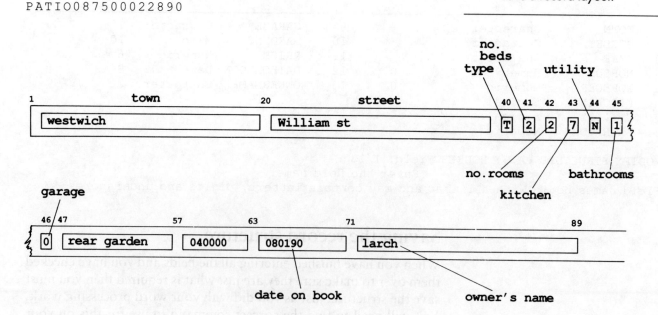

What is the total length of each record?
What makes the difference in the record lengths?

Now re-read this last section and your own manual. Then carefully set out a record description for the file HOUSES and save it.

ENTERING RECORDS INTO A DATABASE FILE

Now you have 'set up' a framework for entering records into your database file, and it is time actually to 'put in' your records. This is the most time-consuming activity with a computerised database system, and the thought of having to enter all the records often puts people off using one. But once the job is done, the benefits in terms of the speed with which data can be accessed and records amended far outweigh this initial slog. So persevere!

For the purposes of learning how to use a computerised database, it is not necessary to enter a lot of records. About 15 or 20 carefully chosen records will do to practise with.

Setting up a database file

If you finished working after saving your record format and switched off your computer, you will now need to load your software again and then set up the correct database file to work on.

TO DO

Get your software loaded and set up ready to **enter** or add records to the database file HOUSES.

You may need to use commands like **update** and **append** (add on) for this. Ask for help if you need to.

Entering a record

CURSOR ← →	UP DOWN	DELETE	Insert Mode : Ins
: Char ← →	: Field ↑ ↓	:Char : Del	: Exit/Save : ^End
: Word : Home End	: Page : PgUp PgDn	: Field : ^Y	: Abort : Esc
	: Help : F1	: Record : ^U	: Memo : Home

```
TOWN
STREET
TYPE
NOBEDS
NORECEP
KITCHEN        ?
UTILITY        ?
BATHROOMS
GARAGE
GARDENS        memo
PRICE

APPEND (<a; >; HOUSES; rec : EOF/16 : :
```

You should have now been able to get to the point where you are provided with a layout on the screen for you to enter your first record. The one for dbase, shown above, displays the help which is available at the top of the screen. Highlighting (not shown here) indicates the size that has been chosen for the fields. If you try to enter the wrong type of data, or too much data, into a field then you hear a warning noise and a message is displayed on the screen. With dbase, as you fill up one field the cursor automatically moves on to the next – so if you don't listen and watch what you are doing, you can end up with the wrong data in the wrong fields!

TO DO

Try entering some records into your database file. This is what it might look like when one entry has been made.

```
┌──────────────────────┐  ┌──────────────────────┐  ┌──────────────────────┐  ┌──────────────────────────┐
│ CURSOR ←→            │  │      UP    DOWN      │  │ DELETE               │  │ Insert Mode : Ins        │
│ : Char ←→            │  │ : Field  ↑     ↓     │  │ :Char : Del          │  │ : Exit/Save : ^End       │
│ : Word : Home End    │  │ : Page : PgUp PgDn   │  │ : Field : ^Y         │  │ : Abort : Esc            │
│                      │  │ : Help   :   F1      │  │ : Record : ^U        │  │ : Memo : Home            │
└──────────────────────┘  └──────────────────────┘  └──────────────────────┘  └──────────────────────────┘
```

```
TOWN         GREENSIDE
STREET       GARDEN RD
TYPE         D
NOBEDS       4
NORECEP      3
KITCHEN      Y
UTILITY      Y
BATHROOMS    2
GARAGE       2
GARDENS      memo
PRICE        205000
DATEONBOOK   02/12/90
OWNERNAME    MATHEWS

APPEND (<a;>; HOUSES; rec: EOF/16 : : Caps
```

Make sure that you find out how your system responds to items which are too long or of the wrong type. Find out how much of what you enter is checked by the program, and what error messages you get if you do something wrong. It is much easier to understand error messages when you know what you have done wrong to cause them!

TO DO

Make sure that you have entered all the records on to the HOUSES file from the Appendix and that you have saved them. You should have 16 records on your file.

You should now be able to:

☐ set up a database file

☐ enter or append records to a database file, taking notice of any warnings and correcting the information so the data is entered accurately.

Adding, deleting and amending records

Once you have built your database file, you will be able to make changes to it at any time. The instructions for making alterations vary from one database package to another, so the best thing is to look them up in your manual and practise using them on a test database before you start building and using a real one. It is also a good idea to make a backup copy of all your database files on a regular basis, and particularly before you intend to make any changes to them.

TO DO

Make a backup copy of the database file HOUSES.

Call it HOUSES2. (Ask your teacher, or look in your manual, if you need reminding how to copy a file.)

There are three kinds of change that you can make to a file.

Adding extra records: you can add extra records to your database file at any time. For instance, as more houses come on to the market they will be added on to the estate agent's file of houses for sale.

Deleting records: the record for a house that is sold, or taken off the market by the seller, is removed from the file. The database package will 'mark' the space used by that record for re-use, so that the space taken up by the file on disk is always kept to a minimum. (Some database packages do not immediately remove the record, however, so that if you delete a record by mistake you can still 'rescue' it. Usually the record is only 'lost' when the program is 'shut down' – one reason why you must always come out of a database program properly and never just remove the disks and switch off without exiting the program.)

Amending records: quite often the details of one or more fields in a database record need to be changed. For example, if you are using a database to store names and addresses, you will want to alter the address fields when someone moves house. This again is simple to do: you only have to call up the appropriate record and alter the contents. Do remember to save the record again when the changes have been made!

'Amend' means 'alter' or 'change'.

'Delete' means 'get rid of'.

TO DO

Make the following alterations to your database file HOUSES.

1 Add a record for the following house, which has just come on the market:

Semi-detached Victorian property at 45 Weston Avenue, Southwich. 5 bedrooms, 2 bathroom, kitchen, utility, dining room, sitting room and study. Owners Mr and Mrs Green. Price: £185 000. Put on sale 23 March 1991. Gardens good size but need attention, mainly left to grass with a few fruit trees and an old shed in need of repair. Wooden double garage.

2 Change the price for the house belonging to Mr Firsley to £75 000.

3 Delete the record for the house costing £189 950 in Spinney Avenue, Chapel Holme, as it has been sold.

4 Change the record for the Lovesons' house to leave out the current use, as they do not wish this to be known.

5 Add in the fact that the house in Acorn Drive, Westwich, has a second bathroom. Also change its price to £170 000 – a typing error has been made!

Finding the record you want: indexes

You have seen how each record in the database is given a number. These numbers correspond to the order in which the records were entered: the first record entered will be number 1, the second 2 and so on. If you have 20 records and then you add a new one, this will become 21. If record number 18 is deleted, the other records are 'moved up': record 19 now becomes record 18, and so on.

If you want to see the records in the order in which they are kept on the database file, you simply print out a list of the records.

If your database file contains hundreds of records, you can't rely on finding a given record simply by the number it has been given. You can search the database to find the correct record and then note down its number. Or, even better, you can index the database in some way.

Earlier on (pp. 87–8) you read about how information is classified and indexed to make it easier for people to find what they want. Exactly the same methods can be used when setting up a computerised database. With the estate agent's file you have been using, particular records will usually need to be 'pulled out' for one of two reasons:

- a buyer has come in and wants details on certain types of house within a price range – in this case every query is likely to be different and so a search will need to be made through the file, just as it would in an office filing cabinet

- there is a need to change details on the file – the houses are likely to be known by the owners' names; to search for a particular owner could be difficult and time-consuming unless the records are indexed in alphabetical order of the names.

An index allows people and computers to find things more quickly.

Your database package should allow you to set up an index to each database file, so that you can request a particular record to be displayed simply by typing in the details of a single field, rather than the number or entire contents of a record. Computers work fast – it is quite amazing to see how quickly a particular record can be found from just one piece of information.

TO DO

Set up an index for your HOUSES database file based on the surname field, so that the records can be accessed in alphabetical order of owner. Try finding out the following:

1 Which is the house owned by the people called Catchmerl?

2 Where do the Hopsleys live?

When you ask the database program to build an index, or set up an index for a file, it does just that, it quickly goes through all the records, not moving them around but keeping a list for itself. The list shows which record is where in index order, so that the program can **retrieve** any individual record very quickly indeed.

You saw earlier that one of the most important things with databases is deciding exactly what information needs keeping and how this information is going to be used and accessed. If this is done carefully before the database file is set up then the whole system will work smoothly. But sometimes people decide to use the data on a file for some quite new purpose, and may ask for the database file to be **re-indexed** or re-sorted into a different order. With a manual system this could take days or weeks, but on a computerised system it is quite easy.

TO DO

See if you can re-index your database on price of property.

Right at the beginning of the book the things that computers were 'good at' were described: dealing with large amounts of data was one of them, and performing routine tasks quickly was another. Computerised databases really show how this is done.

SEARCHING A DATABASE FILE

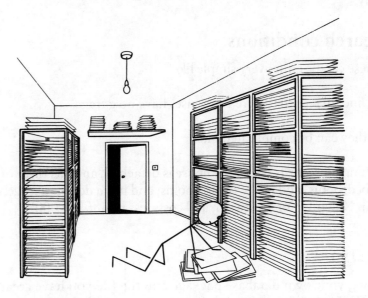

One of the main reasons for needing to keep large amounts of data is so that we can find out things when we want them as quickly and as efficiently as possible. For example, a customer comes in to the estate agent's office and says she is interested in a detached house for a price of between £100 000 and £150 000. How does the estate agent find out what properties he has on his books which meet the customer's requirements?

All the estate agent needs to do is to build a **search** condition for the database program to carry out. He needs to specify two things:

- the contents of the 'type' field must be D for detached, and
- the contents of the 'price' field must be between (and including) 100 000 and 150 000.

TO DO

Find out how to search a data file using your database software. (Look at your manual or ask your teacher.)

You will probably find that the following mathematical symbols are used to help to define search conditions:

- \> means **greater than:** >100 means over 100
- < means **less than:** <50 means under 50
- \>= means **equal to or greater than:** >= 600 means 600 or more
- <= means **equal to or less than:** <=55 means 55 or less
- <> means **not equal to:** <> 0 means any figure or value other than 0.

Also remember that alphabetically A comes before B, and the program therefore sees A as < B (and so on through the alphabet).

Finally, remember that the program will check for things which are *exactly* the same. So if you search for a name in small letters, it will only be found if it was typed into the original record in small letters. This will only *not* be true if your database package is **case-independent** – in other words, if it treats capital and small letters in the same way.

Search conditions

These can be either very simple like:

'find all records where the houses have no garage'

or they can be complicated like:

'find all records where the house is detached, and has three or more bedrooms, and has two bathrooms, and has a double garage, and is in Newtown or Westwich, and costs less than £150 000'.

Notice that in the complicated example the words *and* and *or* keep appearing. When you are building search conditions you have to be careful to use these words correctly.

TO DO

Using your own database package and the file you have created on HOUSES, build search conditions to answer the following questions.

1 Have you any semi-detached properties in Westwich for less than £100 000?

2 I am looking for a house with two bathrooms and four bedrooms to cost between £200 000 and £349 000 in the area – what have you got?

3 How many properties are there for sale in Westwich?

4 Which properties have got no garage?

5 How much does that house for sale in Shrewbridge Road, Southwich, cost?

6 What have you got in the way of cheap properties, say less than £60 000?

7 I need somewhere with a few acres of land – more than two, say, but less than twenty. I'm willing to pay a fair bit. What have you got to offer me?

SORTING

When using a database program you may notice a much slower **response time** than with your word processor. The response time is the time that it takes for the computer to respond back to you after you have given it an instruction. The reason is that a database manages far more data than does a word processor, which generally deals with only one document at a time.

Sometimes you will want to **sort** your records into some type of order based on the contents of one or more fields. For example, you might want to produce a list of all your friends in alphabetical order from a names and addresses database file. Or you might want separate lists of names and addresses in alphabetical order for all those friends who live in the British Isles and all those living abroad, so that you can send Christmas cards out.

This is another job that could take a very long time if it had to be done manually. With a computerised database it can be done in seconds, the actual time taken depending on the number of records in the database file and the power of the machine you are using.

Like search conditions, **sort conditions** can be simple, such as:

'sort all the records in the HOUSES file into order by price'

or complicated, such as:

'sort all the records on the HOUSES file into order based on the type of house, the number of bedrooms and the price'.

TO DO

Try a simple sort command for the HOUSES file. Sort all the records into order by price, with the highest-priced houses first.

PRINTING OUT

When you sort or search through a database file you can usually have your results either shown on the screen or printed out.

Often you only need to look at an individual record, and perhaps to see this on the screen is sufficient. But when you need things listing in order or you want a list of particular records you need to produce a hard copy or print-out of the results. If you have not already done so, try getting the results of the last TO DO exercises listed out using your printer.

Do make sure that, just as for the word processing package you used, the printer is set up and can understand the commands being sent to it from the database software. Get someone to help you with this.

You should now be able to:

☐ index and re-index a database file of records

☐ sort and search a file of records

☐ display the results of search and sort conditions on the computer screen or print them out.

BITS AND PIECES ON DATABASES

Changing the record structure

In the last section you read about how to change the records on a database file by adding, amending or deleting records and by changing the index to the records. Sometimes, though, you may have to actually change the structure of the records, perhaps to add new information or get rid of redundant information. For example, when postcodes were introduced a new field to contain the postcode information had to be added to any record structure where addresses were kept.

In a manual system this could be quite difficult to do. You might have to design completely new record cards, and then copy all the records on to the new set of cards.

On a computerised system this is usually a fairly simple process. You just have to **amend the record structure** and then get the database package to transfer data over to the new format. If new data items need to be added individually to each record then you will still have to do this. But you won't need to copy out all the existing data as well – the computer will do that for you.

TO DO

Find out how to modify or alter a record structure using your own database management package.

Make a copy of your HOUSES file. Then try altering the record structure to:

1 add a new field to say whether an offer has been made on the property

2 delete the field showing the date when the house went on the market.

Why should I use a computerised database package?

If you have ever had the job of wading through large amounts of data of any type searching for the one piece you want, you won't need convincing of the benefits of a computerised database package!

Society today needs to be able to use as much information as possible. For example, just think of the huge amounts of information that the Drivers Vehicle Licence Centre must hold, and how very quickly the police can discover who owns a particular vehicle – only possible because the system is computerised!

To use information effectively we need to be able to classify and group it in ways which make it easy to analyse. Sometimes we don't know what is the best way to organise the information until we try one method and find it doesn't work! All of this can be very time-consuming and laborious work – just the sort of thing which computers were created for.

When a new computerised database system is being set up, specialist professionals generally install it and run it in parallel with the manual system for some time to check that it does do all that is required and that no data gets lost. Once the computerised system has proved itself then – so long as sensible security and backup procedures are followed – the manual system can be got rid of.

SECURITY

If you are keeping large amounts of information on a computerised database, you need to be aware that it must be made secure, and kept that way – just as filing cabinets and doors to filing rooms need to be kept locked. With a computerised system, as with any other, you need to protect the stored information from access by unauthorised users. You also need to ensure that you are complying with the Data Protection Act (see page 60).

There are many ways to prevent access to a computerised database system. These range from locking the computer up or putting a 'lock' on the keyboard to the use of pass names and security codes to prevent access to certain files or records. The amount of security you can build in will depend on the database package you have, so if this is of

---

great importance then look at what is available before you buy. You can now buy add-on pieces of software which have been written to perform security tasks, so perhaps you need to look at these.

Finally, don't forget that when you take backups of your database files, these must be kept secure too.

9 · SPREADSHEETS

In the last two chapters you saw how two types of software packages are used. Both of these deal with words. So what about figures?

The answer lies in **spreadsheets** – sometimes called electronic blackboards. These are used in a whole range of business calculations.

WHAT ARE SPREADSHEETS USED FOR?

Spreadsheets have been around for a long time, and have been used mainly by accountants. As the name suggests, they were simply a means of spreading figures over a sheet of paper and carrying out calculations on them. What we are dealing with in this chapter are **computerised spreadsheet packages**. The first computerised spreadsheet package was called VisiCalc and was launched in 1979. This has been followed by hundreds of similar products, such as As-Easy-As, Lotus 1–2–3 and SuperCalc.

Traditionally spreadsheets have been used for preparing financial accounts and other similar calculations involving money. Today they are used for a whole range of jobs, from producing plans on the use of staff hours to geological analysis. For many people who find working with numbers difficult, using spreadsheets has made life very much easier!

TO DO

Make a list of all the things which you have to do which involve calculations and displaying figures.

The list could include things like working out a weekly budget, planning the costs of a holiday or shopping list, or preparing the accounts for a club or local group.

WHAT DOES A SPREADSHEET LOOK LIKE?

Putting it very simply, a spreadsheet package produces on the computer screen a grid made up of rows and columns. Each space on the grid is called a **cell**, and is referred to by the **row** and **column** numbers that identify it. The diagram shows the layout of a typical blank spreadsheet.

E1:				columns		cell E1		ready
	A	**B**	**C**	**D**	**E**	**F**	**G**	**H**
0					**column**			
1		**row**						
2								
3								
4								
5								
6								
7								
8		**example**						
9								
10								

In this spreadsheet the rows are numbered 1, 2, 3, 4, 5 ... and the columns are lettered A, B, C, D ... and so on.

The cell in the top left-hand corner is referred to as **cell A1**, and the cell with the word 'example' in is cell B8.

Spreadsheets can be very large – it is possible to go up to column 254 and row 8192! – and what you see on your computer screen at any moment is simply part of the overall spreadsheet. Moving the cursor allows you to view different parts of a large spreadsheet very quickly. The screen gives what is known as a **window** on to the spreadsheet. This of course is much easier than trying to deal with lots of pieces of paper all stuck together!

Here is an example of a spreadsheet which has been used to create a shopping list.

	A	B	C	D	E	F	G	H
1								
2								
3	ITEM		COST PER ITEM		NUMBER OF ITEMS			TOTAL COST
4								
5	bread		0.45		2.00			0.90
6	sausages		0.88		1.00			0.88
7	potatoes		0.65		1.00			0.65
8	oranges		0.12		4.00			0.48
9	lamb chops		0.89		4.00			3.56
10	coffee		2.99		1.00			2.99
11	flour		0.90		1.00			0.90
12								
13	Total cost of shopping 10.36							

A spreadsheet is made up of cells. Each cell is identified by the column and row it is in.

TO DO

Look at the shopping list spreadsheet, and identify the following:

- the title line
- a column containing the *names* of items
- a column containing *numbers* of items
- a column containing prices
- a column containing the results of a calculation
- a cell containing a total.

Now load the software package which you are going to use and find out how to get to the point where you have a blank spreadsheet on your screen, ready for you to enter information into it.

WHAT CAN GO INTO A SPREADSHEET?

Having looked at the shopping list spreadsheet, you will have realised that there is a whole range of items that can be entered into cells on the spreadsheet.

Characters or labels (literals)

The title and the names of items in the shopping list example are words which have been entered into cells on the spreadsheet. These are known as **literals** or **text** – exactly what you type is put into the cell, and no calculations can be done using them. The usual way to enter a literal is to move to the cell where you want it entering and then simply type in the contents.

Notice that in the shopping list spreadsheet some of the text is centred in the cell, some is left-justified and some right-justified. Also notice that the contents of a cell do not have to fit the size of the cell on the screen – all of the heading was entered into cell A1.

You can move around a spreadsheet in two ways:

- you can use the cursor keys (or a mouse) to move the highlighted area on the screen to the cell you require, or
- you can move directly to the cell you want, usually by entering the cell reference and using one of the function keys.

TO DO

Find out by using your manual, or by asking, how to enter literals or text into your spreadsheet.

Then copy in the text from the shopping list spreadsheet. Make sure you know how to justify or centre the contents of a cell.

There are three ways of correcting any mistakes you make when entering information into a spreadsheet:

- you can use the backspace or delete key (just as you would normally make corrections) *before* you enter the information
- you can re-enter the correct words by overwriting the cell contents
- you can delete the cell contents altogether if they have been entered in a cell which you want blank.

TO DO

Try using the different ways of correcting mistakes described at the foot of page 111.

Numeric cell contents

The price and quantity of each item in the shopping list spreadsheet have been entered as numbers. These are simple to put in and the spreadsheet program will automatically position them. Notice that you cannot enter a comma in a number; for example, 10,234 must be entered as 10234 – *without* the comma. Figures that contain decimal places must be entered using a full stop for the decimal point: 12.45, for example. A number like 12.234567 may be shortened automatically by the software to 12.23 if the program is only set up to cope with two decimal places.

If you are entering money in pounds and pence, don't try to enter the pound symbol or a p for pence. Spreadsheet programs cannot be used to perform calculations on cells which include symbols like these in their contents. If you like, you can add the £ signs in later, when all the figures and calculations have been stored in the spreadsheet.

TO DO

Look up the default setting for decimal places in your spreadsheet. Find out how to change this setting to cater for different numbers of decimal places.

TO DO

Now enter the figures in columns C and E of the shopping list example into your spreadsheet.
Why do you think columns B and D have been left blank?

Calculations or formulae

The figures shown in column H of the shopping list spreadsheet have been obtained by multiplying the cost of an item by the number of items. In this example it would not be too difficult to work these out in your head. But why bother? You can get the computer to do it for you.

Instead of entering a number or words into a cell, you can enter **formulae** or calculations that you wish to be made using the contents of certain cells. To take an example, the contents of cell H5 are obtained by multiplying the contents of C5 by E5 – i.e. $0.45 \times 2 = 0.90$ (C5 $\times$ E5 = H5).

Entering a formula into each of the cells from H5 to H11 could take as long as doing the calculations. So to make life easier we can put the formula into cell H5 and then copy it into each of the cells H6 to H11. The software changes the formula to suit the cell it is in; for example, H7 would contain the formula C7 $\times$ E7.

TO DO

Using your own spreadsheet package, enter the correct formula into cell H5. Then copy it to cells H6 to H11. Symbols used in calculations are given at the top of the next page.

Usually the symbols used in calculations are as follows:

+ for add
– for minus
/ for divide and
* for multiply

You will have to enter an extra symbol before the formula, to show that it is a formula and not a literal. The symbol *before* a formula in Lotus is +, in Microsoft Works =.

Whenever you have a formula which uses several symbols, you need to indicate which bit of the formula to work out first by using brackets. For example,

F3*F7 + C8

and

F3*(F7 + C8)

will give different answers.

Sums

One of the pleasures of using a spreadsheet is in using some of the pre-set **functions** to perform calculations. One such feature is the **sum** function. This enables you to calculate the sum of a series of cells by entering a 'sum formula' into the cell where you wish the sum to be shown. Sums can be made of rows or part-rows, of columns or part-columns.

For instance, in the shopping list example, cell H13 would contain sum(H5: H11).

TO DO

Find out how to enter a sum function on your spreadsheet. Put in the sum for cells H5 to H11 in cell H13 on your practice spreadsheet.

Find out what other functions are available on your spreadsheet. Make a note of them for future use.

The shopping list spreadsheet you have just worked on has only a few cells filled in. But imagine the advantages of being able to add up hundreds of figures – such as the total wages bill for a company – with just one simple command. This is the sort of thing which spreadsheet packages are used for – doing lots of routine calculations very quickly.

SAVING YOUR SPREADSHEET

Once you have created your spreadsheet, you need to save it by writing it to a disk. If you do not do this before exiting the spreadsheet software and switching off your machine, all your work will be lost!

To save the contents of a spreadsheet, get to the Main Menu on your spreadsheet package and look for a choice for 'saving' or for 'file'.

Again, you will need to enter a symbol before the function you are using to show that it is a function.

You should now be able to:

☐ load your spreadsheet software
☐ move around your spreadsheet
☐ enter labels, numbers and calculations into cells on a blank spreadsheet
☐ copy the contents of one cell into other cells
☐ correct errors on your spreadsheet
☐ calculate the sum of a row or column
☐ set up the number of decimal places required.

TO DO

Save the spreadsheet you have prepared under the name SPREAD1.

The spreadsheet you are working on at a particular time is called the **worksheet**.

Clearing the worksheet

When you have saved your worksheet you can either exit the spreadsheet package, or prepare to do the next exercise by clearing your screen to give a blank worksheet. To do this you need to give the commands to **erase the worksheet**.

TO DO

Find the commands to use and then erase SPREAD1 from your screen to leave yourself a blank screen ready for the next exercise.

LOADING AN EXISTING WORKSHEET FROM DISK

Often you will want to look at, or change, a worksheet that you had created earlier. When you do this you need to be able to **retrieve** the worksheet from your disk into the computer's memory and back on to the screen.

TO DO

Look up the commands for retrieving a file or worksheet from disk using your software package. Then retrieve the worksheet SPREAD1 so that it is displayed again on your screen.

Change the heading on SPREAD1 to MY SHOPPING LIST. (To change the heading simply move the cursor to the correct cell and type in the new heading, then press Return and watch the heading change on the worksheet.) Now save the new version and clear the screen.

When you come to save the amended worksheet, you will be asked if you want to replace the one which is currently saved on disk. This is to allow you to use the same basic worksheet, which you can change and then save under a different name. This time you do want to replace the existing spreadsheet.

You should now be able to:

☐ save a worksheet to disk
☐ clear the screen of a worksheet
☐ load an existing worksheet from disk
☐ save an edited file to disk under an existing filename.

CHANGING AN EXISTING SPREADSHEET

Now you know how to enter details into a spreadsheet starting with a blank one and have made a minor correction to an existing spreadsheet, it is time to see how different changes can be made to spreadsheets which have been saved to disk.

TO DO

Start with a blank worksheet.

The following table gives details of the expenses of several sales staff working for a company in the month of June.

	No of phone calls	Mileage	Hotel costs in £	Other costs in £
Mr G Marsden	20	210	60	3
Ms J Walker	50	95	20	0
Ms F Jeffries	15	515	200	20
Mr P S Green	35	270	0	0
Mr M Riley	85	600	350	40

Produce a spreadsheet showing the above information.
Save your spreadsheet to disk using the name SPREAD2.

Remember you cannot enter the £ sign with the figures.

Inserting rows and columns

The spreadsheet saved as SPREAD2 is not much use to anyone, as it has no title and there is no heading for one of the columns. If a manual one had been prepared, then the headings and title could only be added if space was available. With a computerised spreadsheet package we can create the space to insert new rows and columns. To do this it is necessary to move the cursor or highlighting to the start of the row or column before which you wish the new row or column to be inserted. If, for example, you want a new row above row 4 then you would position your cursor on cell A4 before giving the 'insert row' commands.

TO DO

Find out what commands you need to give to insert columns and rows. (Try using the menu, look up your manual or ask someone.) Make a note of these.

Now insert a row before row 1 and put in the heading 'SALES STAFF – EXPENSES SUMMARY – JUNE' on to SPREAD2.

Exercise

The best way to learn how to use any piece of software is to try it out, and this is especially true with spreadsheets. Once you have saved a copy of your original to disk then you can make changes to it without worrying about making mistakes, because you always have the original version on the disk.

In this exercise you are going to make a series of changes to SPREAD2.

Use your manual, or ask a colleague or teacher, if you get stuck. But first try finding your way round the menus to make the required changes yourself.

1 Mrs J Jones handed in her claims late. Insert the following row between the details for Ms Jeffries and those for Mr Green:

Mrs J Jones   5   300   200   10

2 The accountant needs to know the total expenses claimed by each member of the sales team. Add columns to show the amounts to be paid for phone calls and mileage for each person, and the total amount of expenses for each person. Give suitable headings to the columns.

To be able to put in the correct formulae you need the following information:

- Phone calls are paid for at 20 pence per call
- The mileage rate is 30 pence per mile
- The hotel and other costs are paid in full.

Do not use the actual amounts for mileage and phone calls in the calculations, but simply the cell address where they are stored. To do this you will need to look up in your manual or ask about **absolute cell values.**

3 Find out how to display data in 'cash format' and show the appropriate data in this way.

4 Mr Marsden made a mistake when he put in his claim – he made 40 phone calls, not 20. Change this information.

5 Your spreadsheet package will have a default setting for the width of the columns. Find out what this is and alter it if necessary so that your spreadsheet layout is clear.

6 Check your spreadsheet against the one shown opposite and then save it under the name SPREAD3.

You should now be able to:

☐ amend the data formats of cells to justify them

☐ display cell contents in a 'cash format'

☐ add new data to an existing spreadsheet

☐ delete data from an existing spreadsheet

☐ replace existing data in a given cell

☐ add new formulae to an existing spreadsheet

☐ set the width of individual cells or columns.

PRINTING A SPREADSHEET

Often the spreadsheet you have produced will not all print on to one piece of paper, and you may have to experiment and print certain sections or ranges of rows and columns at a time. How you do this will depend on what the spreadsheet is designed to show, and whether or

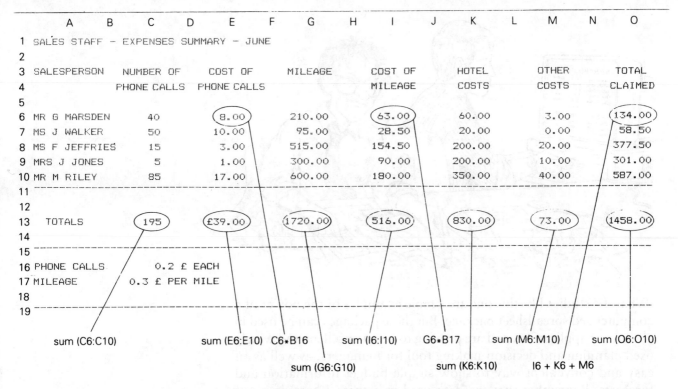

	A	B	C	D	E	F	G	H	I	J	K	L	M	N	O
1	SALES STAFF - EXPENSES SUMMARY - JUNE														
2															
3	SALESPERSON	NUMBER OF		COST OF		MILEAGE			COST OF		HOTEL		OTHER		TOTAL
4		PHONE CALLS		PHONE CALLS					MILEAGE		COSTS		COSTS		CLAIMED
5															
6	MR G MARSDEN	40		8.00		210.00			63.00		60.00		3.00		134.00
7	MS J WALKER	50		10.00		95.00			28.50		20.00		0.00		58.50
8	MS F JEFFRIES	15		3.00		515.00			154.50		200.00		20.00		377.50
9	MRS J JONES	5		1.00		300.00			90.00		200.00		10.00		301.00
10	MR M RILEY	85		17.00		600.00			180.00		350.00		40.00		587.00
11															
12															
13	TOTALS		195	£39.00		1720.00			516.00		830.00		73.00		1458.00
14															
15															
16	PHONE CALLS			0.2 £ EACH											
17	MILEAGE			0.3 £ PER MILE											
18															
19															

sum (C6:C10) sum (E6:E10) C6*B16 sum (I6:I10) G6*B17 sum (M6:M10) sum (O6:O10)

sum (G6:G10) sum (K6:K10) I6 + K6 + M6

not you need to show all the values or simply row and column totals or averages.

TO DO

Try printing out selected rows and columns or sections of SPREAD3. You will need to find the commands for printing. These will be available on your Main Menu.

USES OF SPREADSHEET PACKAGES

One of the most useful features of a computerised spreadsheet is that you can find out what will happen if certain changes are made to perhaps just one of the figures in a table. For example, with SPREAD3 you can find out how much difference it would make to the total expenses claimed if the mileage rate rose to 40p per mile. If a manual spreadsheet was used the whole thing would have to be re-written; with the computerised version, only the formula needs to be changed.

TO DO

Recall SPREAD3 and make a copy of it. Call this SPREAD4.

Alter the cost of mileage to take into account a rise in the mileage rate to 40p per mile.

What happened to the figures in the column when the new formula was entered? Did the 'total expenses claimed' figures alter? Compare SPREAD3 and SPREAD4.

'What if?' studies like this one are simple examples of the power of a computerised spreadsheet package. But these packages can be used in all sorts of applications and are proving to be an excellent and widely used planning and decision-making tool for managers, as well as an easy and convenient way to show simple budget information and forecasts. Remember that the data used in a spreadsheet does not have to be financial – it could be the number of man hours needed to perform a certain job within a factory, or flows of chemicals around a works. The possibilities are almost endless.

This chapter has been a very simple introduction to spreadsheets. If you want to find out more, read your manual or look for text books that just deal with spreadsheets. You may find that the best way to learn more would be to go on a course that specialises in the spreadsheet package that you are going to use.

10 · COMPUTER-AIDED GRAPHICS AND DESK TOP PUBLISHING

In this book you have so far met with three different types of applications software – word processing, database management systems and spreadsheets. This chapter deals with two other common types of applications software, which are perhaps a little more specialised in their use. They are computer-aided graphics software and desk top publishing software.

COMPUTER-AIDED GRAPHICS (CAG)

Graphics software, as the name suggests, is used to produce pictures and diagrams. Many different uses are made of CAG packages and as a result there is a wide variety of such packages on the market, often 'tailored' for particular uses – in fashion design, for example, or in map production or engineering drawing.

The diagram shows the wide range of design activities that make use of CAG software. On the diagram you will notice that CAE (computer-aided engineering), CAD (computer-aided design), CAM (computer-aided manufacturing) and CAAD (computer-aided art and design) are all linked under the main Graphics heading. People

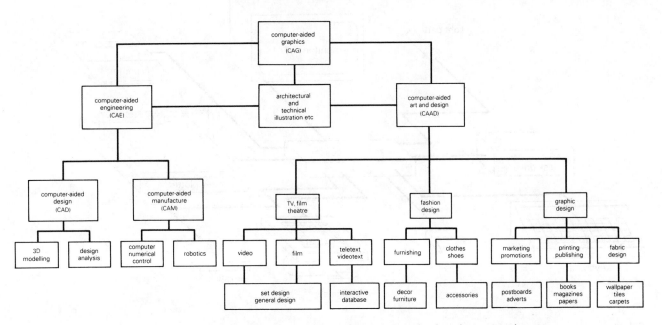

The relationship between CAG and other design applications

working in these fields all need CAG software, but they do need other software too. CAG software may be used to produce a design for a car, for example, but then other software will be used to test the design for engineering problems and to set up a production line to produce the car. The design produced using the CAG software will be saved in such a way that it can be picked up and used by other software packages.

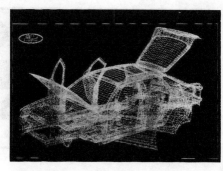

Computer graphics in use in a drawing office in a car manufacturing plant

TO DO

Make a list of examples of the use of CAG software which you have seen, or of areas of work where it could possibly be used. Try to find out how CAG packages benefit the people using them.

Find out whether the people using the software had to have any particular skills to use it.

When you have completed the 'TO DO' activity above you will probably realise that people using a CAG package to design a piece of clothing or an engineering part are using the graphics package as a *tool* – they have the design skills but use the computer because it saves them a lot of time and effort. It lets them see quickly what the effect would be of, say, changing the position of a pocket on a jacket or the height of a heel on a shoe.

The more expensive graphics packages allow three-dimensional images to be shown. They can soon pay for themselves in terms of time saved – for example in allowing an architect quickly to see the effect of changing the slope of a roof in a design for a factory building.

Some examples of graphics used for these types of application are shown in the diagrams.

Hardware needed for CAG systems

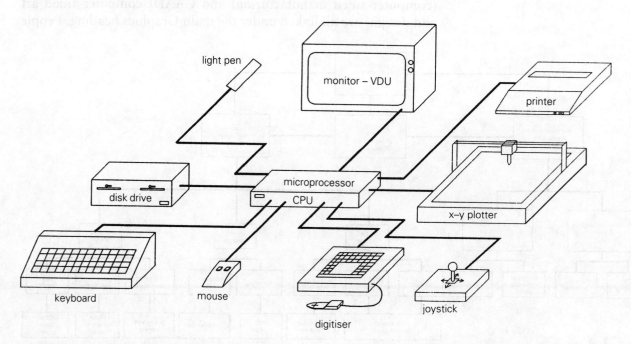

Schematic diagram of a CAG system

In the previous chapters you read about the different types of peripheral devices that are used to build up a computer system for a particular purpose. The diagram on page 120 shows the hardware that could be used with a CAG system – not all the peripheral devices shown would be needed at any one time, however.

Hardware suitable for CAG is often fairly expensive. One reason is that 'pictures' require far more storage and processing space than text or numerical data do, and therefore more powerful machines are needed.

TO DO

Look back through the book and remind yourself of what each of the peripheral devices shown on the diagram does.

How does the computer understand a picture?

In Chapter 3 (page 30), you met the idea that the image on a VDU screen is made up of a series of dots, or pixels. The computer stores and manipulates pictures in the same way – as a series of dots, where the position of each dot on the picture is recorded as a pair of **co-ordinates**. Look at the example on the left.

On a VDU screen, the number of points that can be used as co-ordinates depends on the screen's resolution. The greater the resolution, the larger is the number of points that the screen can accommodate, and the clearer and more accurate is the picture that is produced. If the resolution is poor then the picture may show curves or circles that look 'stepped' (see the diagram).

In the same way digitisers (for input) or printers (for output) will only produce clear images if they are of a suitable quality. Digitisers for CAG must therefore be able to sample at a very high number of points, and dot matrix printers must have a large number of pins in the printhead (see page 33). So it is important that high-quality input/output devices are used with CAG packages – another reason why hardware for CAG is often expensive.

TO DO

Get hold of a copy of the CAG software that you are going to be using and a manual or set of instructions to go with it. Find out what peripheral devices you are going to need, and get to know how these are connected to the main processor. To begin with you will probably use only a mouse and a printer.

Driver software

If you wish to use a peripheral device like a mouse or a digitiser, you have to tell the processor that it is there and how to communicate with it. (Otherwise it cannot pass messages from the mouse to the graphics software, or from the software to a printer.) You do this using **driver software**. This is simply a set of instructions for the processor so that the corresponding peripheral device can be used.

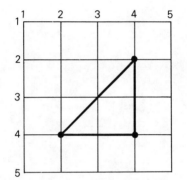

The triangle can be identified by its co-ordinates

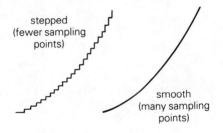

stepped (fewer sampling points)

smooth (many sampling points)

The higher the screen resolution, the more accurate are the pictures.

Unless a driver for a mouse has been installed on your computer, the mouse simply will not work. You will get an error message from the system to tell you what is the matter.

TO DO

Make sure that all the necessary driver software has been installed. Then load the CAG package you are going to use in the same way as you have loaded other packages. Look at any menu that is displayed. You will probably find that 'help screens' are available. Have a look at some of them.

What can you do with a graphics package?

This very much depends on the package you are using, what peripheral devices you can use with it and the standard of the hardware which you have available.

In general, a simple CAG package will allow you to:

- copy shapes from one position to another
- draw straight lines anywhere on the screen, using a variety of thicknesses and types of line
- draw shapes such as rectangles and circles by selecting the shape required and setting the size needed
- edit shapes and lines on an existing drawing by copying, deletion or insertion
- insert saved shapes into other drawings
- move, or 'cut and paste', shapes to new positions
- define the position of a point using co-ordinates
- list files available on a disk (**directory**)
- load previously saved pictures so that they can be edited or printed out
- produce a hard copy of a picture
- save a drawing or picture
- enlarge a particular area of the screen so that greater detail can be added to a drawing.

Some other facilities which are very useful are:

- be able to produce a mirror image of a shape
- produce copies of a shape rotated about a point
- define a scale for plotting on a printer so that various sizes of picture can be produced
- be able to use a range of colours.

Many of the words used above like 'edit', 'load' and 'save' will now be familiar to you from using other software packages such as word processors. Some will be less familiar and it is these that you must start getting to know.

TO DO

Start by getting used to using a mouse, if you have never used one before. You will find that it is a very sensitive device, and you must not move it too quickly. It does not matter what you draw to begin with. Just get familiar with things like how to select different thicknesses and types of line, and how to 'rub out' mistakes or bits you don't like. Then make sure that you can:

- draw straight lines and curves
- save a drawing
- print a drawing
- recall a drawing and edit it.

With CAG software there is absolutely no substitute for the 'hands on' approach. Some people find they really enjoy using this type of software, perhaps more than a database management package. It all depends on the individual: some people are better with words and figures than with pictures.

The important thing with any software package is to make sure that you know what it can do. Then you can decide whether or not it could provide a useful tool to make your life easier – which is after all the whole point of using a computer!

Graphs and charts

In general graphics packages are most widely used by non-specialists in the design field to produce graphs and charts – in other words, to show information in a picture to make it easier to understand. Such things as pie charts, bar charts and line graphs can all be produced using graphics packages.

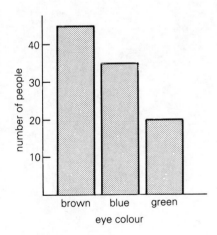

A simple bar chart

If you are not sure what these charts and graphs mean, look at a maths books such as *Work Out Maths* or *Mastering Mathematics* (both published by Macmillan).

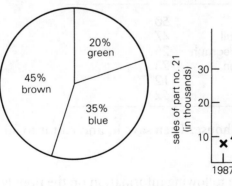

The information in the bar chart displayed in a pie chart

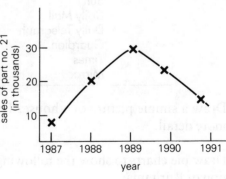

A simple line graph

Recently the facilities to provide charts and graphs have been added into spreadsheet and other types of software, and many integrated packages contain some graphics software. This has made life even easier, as you can now move straight from entering data into a spreadsheet or database to producing diagrams to illustrate their contents with a few simple commands.

TO DO

Look at the spreadsheet and database management software that you have used, and see if these facilities are available in them.

Defining shapes in a CAG package

If you need precise and accurate diagrams, rather than freehand pictures, you have to be able to give the exact points at which each line starts and ends and the angle at which it lies, the size of each circle, and so on. So you need to be familiar with the idea of co-ordinates, and with such terms as radius, diameter, polygon and so forth.

If you really want to be able to do this sort of work and are not familiar with these terms, you will need to look them up in a mathematics book – such things are outside the scope of this book. Then look at your manual to see how to produce accurate shapes.

Getting to know your graphics package

You should now have a basic knowledge of what a graphics package can do. The best thing to do next is to play around with it – we all learn more through play!

This book cannot describe exactly how to produce pictures or graphs, because what you do with a graphics package is very much an individual matter. You might like to try the following exercises, however.

Exercises

1 Draw a bar graph to show the following information:

Sales of newspapers for 11–18 February 1992 at Brown's newsagent's shop (numbers of copies)	
Sun	50
Daily Mail	47
Daily Telegraph	25
Guardian	23
Times	12
Mirror	62

2 Draw a simple picture of a house. Then save it, and edit it to add more detail.

3 Draw pie charts to show the following information on the population of Ruritania:

Percentage of population by age group		
	1970	1990
0–16	15%	29%
17–60	50%	45%
61	35%	26%

DESK TOP PUBLISHING (DTP)

Desk top publishing packages have become one of the most fashionable types of software on the market. They are able to combine pictures and words and can be used to produce a whole range of items, from documents and newsletters to books. The illustration shows a sample page from this book showing how text and pictures are combined using a DTP package to create the finished product.

Inside view of an automated system for storing large numbers of tape cartridges; the robotic arm is selecting a cartridge

robots, who load and unload cartridges as they are required. The reason why tapes and cartridges are used mainly for backups is that information on them can only be read **serially**. That is, it takes longer to find a piece of data than with a disk which can be read **randomly**.

serial order   random order

With **serial access**, data is read one piece after another in physical order. You could say that the players on the left will leave the field in serial order.

With **random access** data can be read in any order at all. The players on the right will go in random order.

There are several other types of magnetic storage but the use of these is limited. **Magnetic card**, for example – as used on cash cards – used to be more common in small office systems. '**Solid-state disks**' are not actual revolving disks; instead, the data is stored on chips, which appear to the processor as a disk. Access is much faster than with revolving disks.

As with input and output devices, the main problem with storage equipment concerns their mechanical parts. With disks and tape the speeds of transfer of information depend on the speed with which the read/write heads can operate and the disks can turn or the tapes wind on. For this reason the main developments in storage technology are in finding ways to reduce **access times** (how long it takes to get hold of a piece of information) and in increasing the capacities of the disks and tapes used.

MAGNETIC STORAGE 41

The advantages of a DTP package are that pictures and words are combined on the screen, and the size and position of diagrams or sections of text can be altered within a few seconds, so that the effect of changes can easily be seen.

DTP is used in book, magazine and newspaper production for

designing and 'making up' pages, where it replaces the old manual techniques of literally 'cutting and pasting'. It is also used for producing company reports or similar documents where graphs, diagrams and pictures need combining with text in order to illustrate points.

Hardware for DTP

A suitable system for using DTP would be similar to the layout shown on page 120 for graphics work. A simple system might consist of just a PC and a laser printer, while a commercial system required to produce a variety of high-quality output would include extra storage, one or more high-quality laser printers, a scanner, the facility to include video images and probably several PCs networked together.

As with graphics, DTP files including pictures or particular layouts take a lot of 'space' to store and work with. So for the sophisticated DTP packages a powerful PC and a hard disk are essential. The more limited packages may not need so much power.

TO DO (1)

Find out why laser printers are usually used with a DTP system. What are the advantages of this type of printer over other printers for DTP?

TO DO (2)

Find out what hardware (peripheral devices and processing power) and software you are going to use, and what facilities are available in the software.

Terms

In order to use a DTP package effectively, you need to be able to understand the terms used. These terms are not used only with DTP packages but are often found also in word processing manuals, printer manuals and in the printing and publishing world in general. They are concerned with the style, size and spacing of characters, words and pages, not with the actual content – that is the writer's job!

Typefaces

Typefaces or fonts are the styles of character used. There are many different ones available – what you use will depend on your software and printer and on the purpose of yout document. Some examples are shown on the right. Notice that in some typefaces, such as Bookman and Courier, the characters have little cross-strokes, called serifs, at the top and bottom of the vertical lines. Other typefaces, such as Helvetica, have no serifs and are called sans serif typefaces ('sans' means 'without').

TO DO

Look at different books, magazines and newspapers, and see if you can spot different typefaces.

Look at the DTP package you are using and see what typefaces are

AvantGarde-Book
AvantGarde-Book Oblique
AvantGarde-Demi
AvantGarde-Demi Oblique
Bookman-Demi
Bookman-Demi Italic
Bookman-Light Italic
Bookman-Light
Courier
Courier-Bold
Courier-Bold Oblique
Courier-Oblique
Helvetica
Helvetica-Bold
Helvetica-Bold Oblique
Helvetica-Narrow
Helvetica-Narrow Bold
Helvetica-Narrow Bold Oblique
Helvetica-Narrow Oblique
Helvetica-Oblique
NewCenturySchlbk-Bold
NewCenturySchlbk-Bold Italic
NewCenturySchlbk-Italic
NewCenturySchlbk-Roman
Palatino-Bold
Palatino-Bold Italic
Palatino-Italic
Palatino-Roman
Σψμβολ
Times-Bold
Times-Bold Italic
Times-Italic
Times-Roman
Zapf Chancery-Medium Italic
✳✳✧✧▼✳✳□✳✧O▼O➝✓

available for you to use. Can you see any which would be particularly suitable for different purposes? – for example:

- an invitation to a wedding
- a brochure for an old-fashioned hotel
- an advertisement for a new computer
- a menu for an expensive French restaurant.

What typeface you choose is up to you. Just as in word processing (pp. 72–3), you will need to consider the height of the characters (measured in points) and whether you want to use proportional or non-proportional spacing, and if non-proportional what pitch you will use.

Page layout

Once you know what typeface you wish to use, you have to decide on a layout for your page(s). To do this you need to work out the margins you want at the top, bottom, left and right of the page and, if you are producing a newsletter, the spacing (or 'gutter') between columns. The diagram shows an example of a page layout – in fact, the one used in this book. (The 'live area' is the area available for filling with text and pictures.)

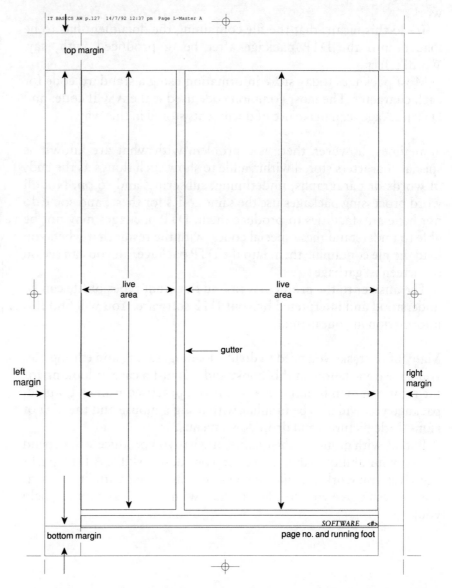

IT BASICS AW p.127 14/7/92 12:37 pm Page L-Master A

top margin

live area   live area

gutter

left margin   right margin

SOFTWARE <#>

bottom margin   page no. and running foot

You have met many of the terms used with page layout already, when you studied word processing packages.

TO DO

Remind yourself what the following mean, and then see if you can find them in your DTP manual:

- Tabs
- justification
- indents
- ruler lines and guide lines.

Loading files to use with DTP packages

When you produce a document using a word processing package and save it, it is stored in a coded form ready for when you next use it. Graphics are stored similarly. Most people using DTP packages produce the text using a word processing package and the pictures using a graphics package (or by scanning the picture in) and then use the DTP software to combine the two and achieve the best layout for the work.

To do this means that the file containing the document has to be loaded into the DTP package after being produced with, say, WordPerfect.

Most packages today store information using a standard code for each character. The most common code used is the ASCII code, and DTP packages can make use of documents stored in this way.

Sometimes, however, there is a problem with what are known as **special characters** stored within a file to show such things as the ends of words or paragraphs, underlining, subscripts and so on. Not all word processing packages use the same codes for these, and some do not have any facilities to produce them. DTP packages may not be able to understand these special codes, with the result that when you load the file containing them into the DTP package, all you can see on the screen is 'garbage'.

The answer to the problem is to find out what types of file can be understood and interpreted by your DTP software. You will find this information in your manual.

Many of the tasks you need to do like loading, saving and editing files you have done before in this book, and it is just a case of looking for the right commands in the manual. If you practised using a graphics package you will also be familiar with using a mouse and the idea of **icons** (little pictures) and drop-down menus.

But, as with graphics, the quality of what you produce will depend less on your ability to use IT than on your design skills. A DTP package saves you work and allows you to try things out with little effort, but it doesn't give you the ideas to start with – it is just a tool to help you.

ASCII stands for American Standard Code for Information Interchange.

Through reading this book you will have learnt about the basics of the hardware and software used in information technology.

If you have followed the book through and completed the exercises, you should now be in a position to decide for yourself how useful IT can be to you. You may decide that you have no use for spreadsheet software, or that you never need to draw pictures. You may also decide that you can't manage without a computer and that word processing is the best thing since sliced bread!

Whatever your decisions, keep an open mind on the use of IT. It isn't just a gimmick or a game – millions of people all over the world now find that life has become easier since they discovered the benefits of IT.

GLOSSARY

analogue   used to describe things which can vary continuously, e.g. analogue wave or clock

applications software   instructions (programs) for computers to carry out a particular job e.g. word processing

arithmetic logic unit (ALU)   the part of the computer's central processor where the work (e.g. calculations) gets done

auxiliary storage   extra storage outside the computer's main memory – also known as backing store

bar code   a type of code consisting of a series of vertical lines of different thicknesses and spacings; used in shops, libraries and so on

bar code reader   an input device used to scan bar codes

bit   the smallest unit of information (abbreviation of binary digit)

byte   a group of eight bits; usually one byte represents one character

central processing unit (CPU)   the part of the computer which is the 'brain' – here instructions are decoded, the hardware controlled and instructions executed; it consists of the control unit, the arithmetic logic unit and the internal memory

computer-aided design (CAD)   the use of computers to aid the design of many types of product; used, e.g., in the fashion industry, engineering and architecture

computer-aided graphics (CAG)   the use of computers to produce graphic design work of any kind

computer-aided manufacturing (CAM)   the use of computers in the manufacturing process of many types of product; used, e.g., in the car industry, the dairy industry and engineering

computer-assisted learning (CAL)   the use of computers to help people to learn; includes tutorial programs, which may be interactive or purely instructional

continuous stationery   fan-folded paper (sometimes multipart) divided into pages by perforations; it is used with line and impact dot matrix printers

cursor   a movable mark on screen which shows where the next character or other input will be displayed

data   general term describing all numbers, letters and symbols; data with meaning becomes information

database   a structured set of records made up of a quantity of information which is usually related; can be manual or electronic/computerised

database management system (DBMS)   software designed for the purpose of managing databases

dedicated computer   a computer set up for one specific purpose (for example, a dedicated word processor)

default   a system- or program-provided option that is used automatically unless an alternative is specified

desk top publishing (DTP)   the use of computer packages which combine text and graphics; used widely for producing high-quality books, reports, handouts etc.

digital   having discrete states

digitising tablet or graphics tablet   a device comprising a flat plate which senses the position of a small pointing unit resting on its surface; when connected to a computer movement of the pointer is picked up, allowing input of lines, marks or data at any point on the screen

disk directory   a listing of details of files stored on a disk

disk/diskette   a small disk coated with magnetic material on which data can be recorded

disk drive   a device which enables data to be written to and read from disks

document   hard copy or soft copy of a complete data file

document reader   an input device which reads marks or characters (usually on special forms)

dot matrix printer   a printer which prints characters from a matrix of dots; output quality depends on the number of dots in the matrix

dumb/unintelligent terminal   a terminal which does not have a CPU; the unit can only send or receive data from the central system

edit   to examine and make changes to displayed data

electronic mail   the electronic transfer of messages/documents to computers over a network

facsimile (fax)   a system of still picture transmission and reception using synchronised scanning at transmitter and receiver

field   a physical space on a data-recording medium which is reserved for one or more related items of data elements, or the data element itself which forms part of a record

file   in general, any organised and structured collection of data

firmware   computer programs which are stored in the ROM of the machine

floppy disk   a thin flexible and portable plastic disk

format   (a) the layout of text on a screen or document; (b) the preparation of a disk for use

gateway   in telecommunications, equipment or software used to interface networks so that a terminal on one network can communicate with a terminal or computer on another network which doesn't use the same 'language'

graphics   a pictorial display

graphics tablet   *see* **digitising tablet**

hard copy   sheet or sheets of paper on which data is represented in human-understandable form

hard disk   a rigid disk which is usually fixed inside the machine; also known as a **fixed disk**

hardware   the physical components of a computer system

high-level language   a programming language which is relatively machine-independent and closer to English

indentation   the positioning of text a number of spaces to the right of the left margin

input device   a unit of hardware from which data is transmitted to the computer

intelligent terminal a terminal which includes a central processing unit

interface generally the connecting link between devices or systems

joystick a control device which moves in two dimensions, providing input; generally used for games

justification formatting text so that lines are of equal length with straight right or left margins; spaces between words are enlarged to allow this

keyboard an input device which is a system of keys

keystroke pressing a single key on a keyboard once

light-emitting diode (LED) an output device which glows when supplied with a specific voltage; commonly used as indicators and display devices which can glow in the dark

light pen a hand-held light-sensitive stylus that detects light from the screen on most VDUs; also used to read bar codes

liquid crystal display (LCD) an output device that reflects light – cannot be used in the dark

local area network (LAN) a computer network which is restricted to a limited geographical area

machine code binary code which is directly understood by the central processing unit

magnetic ink character recognition (MICR) an input device that allows machine recognition of stylised characters printed in magnetic ink

magnetic media data storage materials where the means of storage is provided by a surface layer of magnetic material

magnetic reader an input device which reads magnetic strips on, for example, bank cash cards

mainframe computer a large general-purpose computer with extensive processing, storage and input/output capabilities

memory the part of a computer which receives data in the form of binary digits and stores it for future use

menu-driven software software that requires the operator to make selections from a list

microcomputer a small computer which has a microprocessor as the central unit

microprocessor a central processing unit on a single chip

modem a device which enables transmission of data along the telephone lines; short for modulator/demodulator

monitor a term incorrectly used to refer to a visual display unit; more correctly, it is special software within the operating system

mouse an input device held in the hand which allows input to a computer by sensing movement

near letter quality (NLQ) the quality of text produced by a printer which is close to that produced by traditional printing techniques

network systems connected together to allow communication between them

off-line the state of a peripheral device (q.v.) when it is not in a state to receive or transmit data

on-line the state of a peripheral device (q.v.) when it is able to receive or transmit data

optical character recognition (OCR) an input device that allows input by light-sensing methods

output device a unit of hardware to which data can be transmitted by a computer

overwrite a method of entering text such that it destroys previously entered text in the same place; also known as overtype

page break a code sent to the printer telling it to end a page and start printing on another

parallel transmission the simultaneous transmission of several bits at once; faster than serial transmission (q.v.)

peripheral device any device that is connected to and controlled by the central processing unit of a computer

pitch a measure of horizontal character spacing; the number of characters that are printed per inch

pixel the smallest addressable point on a VDU; one pixel is one of the dots forming the dot matrix of a VDU

plotter an output device that draws lines on paper using pens

point of sale terminal (POS) an input device used to record details about a sale and to transmit stock details to a computer

port the external connection point of peripheral devices to a computer

printer an output device producing characters or graphic symbols on paper

program a set of instructions to a computer to perform a specific task

programming the process of writing programs

puck an input device used with a digitising tablet

random access memory (RAM) read and write computer memory used to store temporary data

read only memory (ROM) memory that can be read repeatedly but cannot be changed

record a collection of related data treated as a unit, each separate item of data comprising the record being known as a field; for example, a person record might contain details of name and address and age

register a memory device that holds a 'single word'

resolution the level of detail visible in any form of display or copy

retrieve the transfer of data stored on magnetic media to RAM so that editing or other processing can take place

ruler line on-screen information about margin and Tab settings

scroll the movement of text up, down or across the screen of a VDU

serial transmission the transmission of data one bit after another

single chip microcomputer a microcomputer that has CPU, memory and input/output fabricated within the same integrated circuit

soft copy screen display of data

software the programs which are used to direct the operation of a computer

source document the originator or master copy of that which is to be processed

spreadsheet a collection of related numerical and textual data in the form of text, numbers and formulae

status line on-screen information concerning the work currently in progress

storage device a unit of hardware that provides the means to store and retrieve data from storage media

system a methodical assembly of parts or operations able to accept input, process it and form output

systems software the software that controls the computer

teletex an internationally agreed standard for the transmission of a wide range of characters; virtually a modern standard of Telex, but 30 to 40 times faster

teletext a means by which textual data is transmitted along with broadcast television pictures; it is a one way system of communication

Telex a telegraph system with its own exchanges that uses teleprinters as terminals instead of telephones

terminal a device used only in on-line mode for communicating with a central computer system; often comprises a VDU and a keyboard

text letters, numbers, words and other symbols used in a document

typeface a named style of type, usually of a specified size

Viewdata this is the international term for services such as Prestel; essentially a two-way information service which allows communication over telephone networks using modified television sets with keyboards or computers with appropriate software

videotex the general term used to describe any system which allows the display of textual information, particularly computer data on a television screen (e.g. Viewdata, teletex, teletext, Ceefax, Oracle)

visual display unit (VDU) a device which displays electronic data, in the form of text or graphics, on a screen

wide area network (WAN) a computer network which covers a wide geographical area

Winchester disk a high-density hard disk

word processing the use of microelectronic equipment in the preparation of textual documents

word processor microcomputer equipment using word processing software which provides text entry and editing facilities

word wraparound a feature of word processing software whereby words which do not fit on a current line are automatically carried over to the next

APPENDIX: DATABASE EXERCISE

DATA FOR HOUSES FILE (page 95)

OWNER   BEECH
TOWN   WESTWICH
STREET   ACORN DRIVE

SEMI-DETACHED, 3 BEDROOMS, 3 RECEPTION, KITCHEN, BATHROOM, SINGLE GARAGE, PRICE £70,000. OFFERED FOR SALE 24/11/90. LONG NARROW GARDEN DIVIDED INTO LAWNED AREA AND PLANTED AREAS, SOME VEG, BY PRETTY WINDING PATH. IMAGINATIVELY LANDSCAPED.

OWNER   BIRCH
TOWN   CHAPEL HOLME
STREET   SPINNEY AVE
PRICE   £189,950

DETACHED 4 BED, 2 RECEP, KITCHEN, BATHROOM, SINGLE GARAGE, BEAUTIFUL WELL-STOCKED GARDENS OF 1/5TH ACRE. OFFERED FOR SALE FROM 28/03/90.

OWNER   CATCHMERL
TOWN   WESTWICH
STREET   DARK LANE
PRICE   £60,000

SEMI-DETACHED 3 BED, 2 RECEP, BATHROOM AND KITCHEN. OUTSIDE SINGLE GARAGE. SMALL BUT WELL-TENDED GARDEN. HOUSE NEEDS MODERNISING AND GARAGE NEEDS ATTENTION. OFFERED FOR SALE FROM 07/12/90.

OWNER   EASTLEY
TOWN   WESTWICH
STREET   BOOTH LANE
PRICE   £35,000

MID TERRACE 2 BED, 2 RECEPTION, BATHROOM AND KITCHEN. SMALL ENCLOSED YARD TO REAR WITH SHED BUT NO GARAGE, FRONT GARDEN SMALL BUT PRETTY, WELL STOCKED WITH BULBS. OFFERED FOR SALE FROM 11/11/90.

OWNER   FIRSLEY
TOWN   MUCKRIDGE
STREET   HOLLY CLOSE
PRICE   £79,000

SEMI-DETACHED, 3 BEDROOM, 2 RECEPTION, KITCHEN, UTILITY AND BATHROOM. SINGLE GARAGE. GARDEN IS SMALL BUT WITH SCOPE TO DEVELOP. MAINLY LAID TO LAWN WITH NATURAL AREAS. OFFERE FOR SALE FROM 04/02/91.

OWNER   HANDIMAN
TOWN   GROOTSEY
STREET   WELL AVE
PRICE   £199,500

DETACHED 4 BEDROOM, 3 RECEPTION, KITCHEN, 2 BATH-ROOMS AND UTILITY ROOM. DOUBLE GARAGE WITH ATTACHED SHED. WELL-STOCKED FRONT GARDEN, REAR LAID MAINLY TO LAWN WITH ROCKERY AND SMALL VEG AREA, MATURE FRUIT TREES. FOR SALE FROM 01/08/90.

OWNER   HOLDON
TOWN   CHAPEL HOLME
STREET   WESTMORLAND TERRACE
PRICE   £59,000

END TERRACE 2 BED, 2 RECEP, KITCHEN AND BATHROOM. NO GARAGE BUT SPACE FOR CAR AT FRONT OF HOUSE ON PAVED AREA. FOR SALE FROM 05/03/89.

OWNER   HOPSLEY
TOWN   SOUTHWICH
STREET   WOLFE STREET
PRICE   £150,000

DETACHED 3 BED, 3 RECEPTION ROOMS, KITCHEN, UTILITY AND 2 BATHROOMS. DOUBLE GARAGE WITH UP AND OVER REMOTE CONTROLLED DOORS. GARDENS SMALL BUT SOUTH FACING AND WELL SHELTERED, IDEAL FOR THE PER-SON WHO WANTS PRIVACY BUT LITTLE GARDENING WORK. FOR SALE FROM 10/07/90.

OWNER   LARCH
TOWN   WESTWICH
STREET   WILLIAM ST
PRICE   £40,000

MID-TERRACE, 2 BEDROOM, SITTING ROOM AND DINING ROOM, KITCHEN AND DOWNSTAIRS BATHROOM. NO GARAGE, REAR YARD. OFFERED FOR SALE FROM 15/01/90.

OWNER   LOVESON
TOWN   EAST GROOTSEY
STREET   FROG LANE
PRICE   £550,000

DETACHED HOUSE WITH LARGE RANGE OF OUTBUILDINGS. STUNNINGLY SITUATED ON THE EDGE OF A LAKE IN A HOL-LOW WHICH IS WELL SHELTERED. 19 ACRES OF POST AND RAIL PADDOCKS LAID TO GRASS. WATER AVAILABLE TO ALL PADDOCKS. CURRENTLY USED AS A STUD FOR WELSH PONIES. MAIN HOUSE HAS 5 BEDROOMS AND 3 BATH-ROOMS, SITTING ROOM, DINING ROOM, BREAKFAST

ROOM, SNOOKER ROOM AND STUDY AS WELL AS KITCHEN, UTILITY AND STORE ROOMS INCLUDING CELLARS. STAFF FLAT ABOVE STABLES WITH 2 BEDROOMS, BATHROOM AND KITCHEN. FOR SALE FROM 28/06/91.

OWNER   OAKLEY
TOWN   WESTWICH
STREET   HALFENDER ROAD
PRICE   £87,500

SEMI-DETACHED, 3 BEDROOM AND BATHROOM, DINING ROOM, LIVING ROOM AND KITCHEN. SINGLE GARAGE TO REAR OF PROPERTY APPROACHED BY ACCESS FROM ALLEY-WAY BEHIND HOUSE. SUN LOUNGE LOOKS OUT OVER PATIO AND DOWN 100 FT OF GARDEN WHICH IS WELL STOCKED WITH PERENNIALS AND FRUIT TREES. FOR SALE FROM 09/11/90.

OWNER   RICHMAN
TOWN   WEST GROOTSEY
STREET   BLACKDEN LANE
PRICE   £350,000

DETACHED COUNTRY PROPERTY IN OWN GROUNDS OF 2 1/2 ACRES WHICH ARE BEAUTIFULLY LANDSCAPED AND INCLUDE AN ORCHARD AND SMALL PADDOCK. FURTHER LAND ALSO AVAILABLE. 3 STABLES, TACK ROOM AND SMALL HAY BARN. HOUSE ITSELF HAS EXPOSED TIMBERS AND DATES BACK TO 17TH CENTURY. THERE ARE 5 BED-ROOMS, 4 RECEPTION ROOMS, 3 BATHROOMS, A KITCHEN AND UTILITY ROOM, DOWNSTAIRS WASH ROOM AND A SEP-ARATE OUTSIDE LAVATORY. THE GARAGE PROVIDES SPACE FOR 3 CARS AND A HORSE TRAILER. FOR SALE FROM 29/07/90.

OWNER   SONDWELL
TOWN   GROOTSEY
STREET   MAIN ROAD
PRICE   £210,000

DETACHED 4 BEDROOM, 2 BATHROOM HOUSE OF CHARAC-TER. NATURAL WOOD AND BRICK FINISHES. LIGHT, AIRY AND SPACIOUS. NEEDS SEEING. DOWNSTAIRS 3 RECEPTION ROOMS, HALL, UTILITY AND CLOAKROOM. OUTSIDE GAR-DENS OF APPROX 1/4 ACRE WITH DETACHED DOUBLE GARAGE INCORPORATING SHED. GARDENS HAVE MATURE TREES AND FACE SOUTH AND WEST. AVAILABLE FOR SALE FROM 13/05/91.

OWNER   SPRUCE
TOWN   SOUTHWICH
STREET   ENDSLEIGH AVE
PRICE   £91,000

2 BEDROOM BUNGALOW, IDEAL RETIREMENT HOME WITH 2 RECEPTION ROOMS, BATHROOM AND NEWLY REFITTED KITCHEN. GARDENS ARE SMALL BUT WELL-TENDED WITH ROCKERY AND WELL-STOCKED FISHPOND, FOUNTAIN AND GNOMES. CARPETS AND CURTAINS ALSO AVAILABLE. SIN-GLE GARAGE. FOR SALE FROM 29/04/91.

OWNER   WILLOWSON
TOWN   SOUTHWICH
STREET   SHREWBRIDGE ROAD
PRICE   £197,500

DETACHED 5 BEDROOM, 2 BATHROOM OLD VICTORIAN PROPERTY IN NEED OF SOME MODERNISATION. HAS 3 RECEPTION ROOMS, KITCHEN AND SCULLERY AND OUT-SIDE LAVATORY, COAL HOUSE AND SHED. 2 CAR LEAN-TO GARAGE. GARDENS ARE LARGE, 3/4 ACRE AND HAVE POTENTIAL. INTERESTING PROPERTY WITH SCOPE FOR DEVELOPMENT INTO THE IDEAL FAMILY HOME.

OWNER   YEWLEY
TOWN   GROOTSEY
STREET   MILL LANE
PRICE   £210,000

DETACHED 4 BEDROOM HOUSE IN PLEASANT WELL-STOCKED SOUTH-FACING GARDENS. THE GARDENS INCLUDE SEVERAL MATURE TREES INCLUDING A WALNUT. THERE ARE 3 RECEPTION ROOMS, ONE OF WHICH HAS FRENCH WINDOWS LEADING ON TO THE PATIO AT THE REAR OF THE HOUSE. 1 BATHROOM, 1 SHOWER ROOM AND KITCHEN AND UTILITY. FOR SALE FROM 23/05/91. DOUBLE GARAGE (ATTACHED).

INDEX